NO MORE FEAR

NO MORE

REVISED
&
EXPANDED

FEAR

YOU HAVE THE MIND OF CHRIST

JOEL OSTEEN

Created and assembled for Joel Osteen Ministries by
Breakfast for Seven
breakfastforseven.com

Printed in the United States of America.

For additional resources by Joel Osteen, visit JoelOsteen.com.

CONTENTS

NO
MORE
FEAR

FOR GOD
HAS NOT GIVEN
US A SPIRIT
OF FEAR,
BUT OF POWER
AND OF LOVE
AND OF A
SOUND MIND.

2 Timothy 1:7 (NKJV)

Introduction

We all feel fear. It's part of life. But that doesn't mean you're weak or that you don't have faith. Even the most faithful face fear — especially in today's world with wars, natural disasters, sickness, an uncertain economy or future. These events try to change who we are — from peaceful to panicked, from trusting to troubled.

But David said in Psalm 23:4 (NKJV), *"Though I walk through the valley of the shadow of death, I will fear no evil. . . ."* He didn't say he'd avoid the valley. He said, "I will not fear." That's the kind of faith we need today — not faith that avoids the fire, but faith that stands in the middle of it and says, *"God is with me. I will not fear."*

Fear may knock, but you don't have to let it in. Let faith answer. When the "what ifs" come — *What if something goes wrong? What if I fail? What if it happens again?* — you remind yourself: *God is my Shepherd. He's got me covered.* You're not doing this alone. God is watching over you, fighting your battles, guiding your steps.

The Scripture says in 2 Timothy 1:7 (NKJV), *"For God has not given us a spirit of fear, but of power and of love and of a sound mind."* That spirit of power is in you. You can't be passive and expect fear to go away. You have to rise up and say like David in Psalm 27:1 (NKJV), *"The LORD is my light and my salvation; whom shall I fear?"*

I didn't title this book *No More Fear* because you'll never feel afraid again. I wrote it so that you don't let fear control you anymore. I believe you're going to take back ground that fear has stolen. You're going to see anxiety lift, confidence return, and courage rise up.

Yes, there are dark valleys. But those valleys are not your destination. Keep walking. Don't let fear trap you. Don't let it talk you out of your dreams, your joy, your purpose. You are not here by accident. God chose you for this time. He's put strength in you that's stronger than the storm.

Your destiny is too great, your calling too important, and your future too bright to live in fear. Get ready — greater favor, greater influence, greater peace is ahead. And when fear tries to come again, you'll be able to say with boldness, *"I will not fear. My Shepherd is leading me, and I'm walking into everything He has prepared for me."*

Don't worry about anything; instead, pray about everything. Tell God what you need, and thank him for all he has done. Then you will experience God's peace, which exceeds anything we can understand. His peace will guard your hearts and minds as you live in Christ Jesus.

PHILIPPIANS 4:6–7 (NLT)

CHAPTER 1

God Uses Scary Places

Y ou weren't made to coast through life and just stay where you are; you were made to take new ground. And to do that, you have to get out of your comfort zone. What God has in store for you may scare you.

God's dreams for you are bigger than what you can accomplish on your own. There are obstacles ahead of you that you can't overcome by yourself. If you've been comfortable too long, God will shake things up. He'll take you out of what's familiar. He'll remove a friend that you counted on, or put you in a position where you're in over your head. And guess what? You'll find yourself praying like you've never prayed before. You'll do things you wouldn't normally do because you're more focused, more disciplined, more determined to work through whatever it is you are going through. It's uncomfortable. You won't like it. But God will use the scary places to move us into our destiny.

We all like when life is going our way. Our family is happy, business is strong, and everything is right on schedule. We like to be comfortable. We like to have it all figured out. But the truth is, we are at our best when we're a little nervous, a little unsure of how it's going to work out, with a little bit of healthy fear.

When you face things that are unfamiliar, it can be scary. You've defeated some opponents, but when you see your Goliath — something bigger than you've ever faced — it can be intimidating. "God, You know he's twice my size; I can't do this; find somebody else." Like the Israelites, you'll feel like a measly grasshopper compared to the giants in front of you (see Numbers 13:33).

But just as David defeated Goliath with a couple of river rocks (see 1 Samuel 17:40), and just as Joshua and Caleb declared of the giants of Anak, "We can take them!" (see Numbers 13:30), you too have been armed with strength for every battle. God has already equipped you, empowered you, and anointed you. You may feel fear, and that's okay. Fear comes to us all. The key is to do it afraid. Do it in spite of what you feel. Do it in spite of what your mind is telling you.

Don't get talked out of your destiny. God is setting you up to go to a new level. In those scary places, you'll discover strength that you didn't know you had — talent, determination, and perseverance that you didn't think was in you. Remember: We don't grow when everything is going our way; we grow in the scary places.

You may feel fear, and that's okay. Fear comes to us all. The key is to do it afraid. Do it in spite of what you feel.

Say "no more" to fear:

▶ **REFLECTION**

David was taken out of the shepherd fields and moved into the palace. Moses was taken out of the palace and moved into the shepherd fields. The Israelites were taken out of Egypt and led into the wilderness. Scripture is full of people being moved from comfortable places into unknown territory. Has God ever taken you out of your comfort zone into an unexpected place — a scary place where you needed faith, where you learned to lean on Him, where you began to grow?

_____

_____

_____

_____

_____

_____

_____

_____

_____

_____

_____

_____

_____

_____

_____

Start living in faith:

▶ **APPLICATION**

Do your dreams scare you? Do you sense a call of God on your life that is bigger than what you can do on your own? If not, begin to dream again. If so, take the next step toward your destiny even if you have to do it afraid.

▶ **DECLARATION**

God has equipped, appointed, and empowered me to do great things — greater than anything I could do on my own. When I feel fear, I will trust God is always with me!

▶ **PRAYER**

God, use the scary places in my life to propel me into my destiny. Take me out of my comfort zone. I am ready to do what You say I can do, be what You say I can be, and have what You say I can have. In Jesus' name, Amen.

CHAPTER 2

Get Out Of The Nest

When a mother eagle has baby eaglets, she makes a nest for those eaglets. The nest is high on the side of a cliff, away from predators. It's a very comfortable nest, cushioned with leaves and grass and soft branches. For the first part of their lives, the eaglets are content. They haven't a care in the world. When they're hungry, they simply open their mouths, and their mother drops food in. Life is good.

But a few months in, the mother eagle starts removing the soft cushion of the nest. She takes away the leaves and the grass and all the things that make it so comfortable. Now when the eaglets sit, they feel the sticks and branches poking them. So they begin to spend more time outside of the nest. They spend hours on the rocks, bouncing up and down, playing with

It may not be comfortable, but when you stay in faith, you'll discover your wings.

each other. They think they're just having fun, but they're actually developing their muscles.

When the mother knows they're strong enough, she'll push her babies, one at a time, out of the nest and off the cliff. Don't you know if the eaglets could talk, they would say, "What has gotten into Mama? This mother who fed us, loved us, protected us, and made our lives so comfortable is now trying to kill us!" In the nick of time, the mother eagle will swoop down and grab her babies out of the air. She'll return her babies safely to the nest. But just when they start to get comfortable, she pushes them out again. This process repeats until the eaglets finally discover their ability and begin to fly.

The nest the eaglets were in was a blessing for a time. It was necessary. But at a certain point, the nest will no longer be a blessing; it will be a hindrance. The eaglets won't develop their wings in the nest, and neither will you. As much as we like the provision, the protection, and having everything handed to us, that place of comfort limits our ability to soar.

"*As an eagle stirs up its nest, hovers over its young, spreading out its wings, taking them up, carrying them on its wings*" (Deuteronomy 32:11, NKJV), so does God spread His wings and carry you until you are ready to soar on your own. You may not like the stirring of the nest or the feeling of being pushed out of your comfort zone. But that is the sign of God working in your life. It may not be comfortable, but when you stay in faith, you'll discover your wings.

Say "no more" to fear:

▶ **REFLECTION**

The apostle Paul writes to the people of Corinth and explains that they are acting like brand-new believers. He gives the analogy of babies who are still nursing and not yet ready for solid food (see 1 Corinthians 3:1–3). It's so important that we keep growing in our faith step-by-step. Eventually we will get stronger, faith-filled, mature, and ready to receive more from God. How has your faith grown since you first became a Christian?

Start living in faith:

▶ **APPLICATION**

How would you describe the maturity of your faith? Whether you are a brand-new believer or have been on the journey for decades, there is always room to grow. Think about the big steps of faith you've taken or are being prompted to take in this season of your life. You've been graced by God to move forward into your destiny. Sometimes, those faith steps look more like leaps!

▶ **DECLARATION**

God has given me all that I need to succeed in life. He wouldn't be stirring the next unless He knew it was my time to fly. I am growing and reaching for my destiny. I am ready to soar.

▶ **PRAYER**

God, thank You for believing in me. Thank You for wanting more for my life. Thank You for the gentle (and not-so-gentle!) ways that You help me discover my wings. Thank You for working in my life and helping me fly. In Jesus' name, Amen.

CHAPTER 3

Beauty For Ashes

When my father died in 1999, I knew I was supposed to step up and pastor the church. He had asked me for years to help him in the pulpit, but I didn't think I could do it. I was comfortable behind the scenes, and I was good at what I did. I didn't want to have to stretch, to get up in front of people, to do something I had never done before.

All the "what ifs" came flooding into my thoughts: *What if you try and fail? What if nobody comes? What if people don't like you? What if you let your father and his legacy down?* It's easy to talk yourself out of God's dream for you because it is so much bigger than your own.

There were times early on when I had to hold on to the podium, I was so afraid. All of my thoughts were telling me that I couldn't do it. But it was in that scary place that I discovered talent I didn't know I had. This was always in me, but if God had not pushed me during a scary, vulnerable, uncertain time, I would have never discovered it.

When you come to the end of life, will you have more regrets over the risks you took, or over the risks you didn't take? I'd rather try and fail than play it safe and never know.

Maybe you're where I was — you've been through a loss, a disappointment, something you don't understand. It took the wind out of your sails. You've lost your passion; there's nothing in front of you that excites you. You're breathing but not living.

Get ready.

Isaiah 61:3 (TLB) says, *"To all who mourn in Israel he will give: beauty for ashes; joy instead of mourning; praise instead of heaviness. For God has planted them like strong and graceful oaks for his own glory."*

God is going to do for you what He did for me. He's going to take that dark hour and use it to launch you into a new level of your destiny. What you've lost is not the end; it's a new beginning. God doesn't waste anything. This season is preparing you for where He's taking you. He has beauty for those ashes, joy instead of mourning, praise to replace your despair. He's about to bring new opportunities, new relationships — things so amazing that you will feel intimidated by them. Don't shrink back. Take the risk. Step into the new. Let Him make beauty from the ashes.

To all who mourn in Israel he
will give: beauty for ashes; joy
instead of mourning; praise
instead of heaviness. For God
has planted them like strong and
graceful oaks for his own glory.

ISAIAH 61:3 (TLB)

Say "no more" to fear:

▶ **REFLECTION**

Jesus says that in this life there is one guarantee — you will have trouble. You will have trials and sorrow. None of us will make it through life without facing challenges of many kinds. But in John 16:33, Jesus encourages us to cheer up, for He has overcome the world. He has overcome all that has and all that will come against you. God wants you to dream again, to laugh again, to love again, and to believe again. Think of a time in your life when God transformed your ashes into beauty, your mourning into joy, or your troubles into good cheer. Perhaps it was even a time when your situation didn't change, but your heart did.

_____

_____

_____

_____

_____

_____

_____

_____

_____

_____

_____

_____

Start living in faith:

▶ **APPLICATION**

Are you in a season of loss, pain, disappointment? Are you having trouble understanding what God is doing? Know this: God is not done with you. What lessons are you learning in this season that hint at your destiny? When you feel that passion stirring, step out. Take a risk. Be willing to try. Even if you fail, you'll be one step closer to where God is calling you next.

▶ **DECLARATION**

I am excited for my future. God is transforming my mourning into gladness. He is restoring unto me all that has been lost. His mercies are new every morning. I feel passion stirring in me again.

▶ **PRAYER**

God, I surrender these ashes to You. You are the potter; I am the clay. I love You. I trust You. You promised beauty for ashes, and You always keep Your Word. In Jesus' name, Amen.

CHAPTER 4

Fuel For Your Faith

Anyone who knows me knows that I'm constantly talking about how God healed my mother from terminal cancer in 1981, how He gave us the Compaq Center, and how He helped me make it through the loss of my father. The reason I'm always talking about those things is because I need that fuel for my faith. I need to remember what God has done — how He showed out in my life — so I won't shrink back when new opportunities come my way.

When you keep the right attitude, God will work all things for your good (see Romans 8:28). When you face dreams that look too big and obstacles that seem insurmountable, look back and remember how God brought you through in the past. Remember how He made a way when you didn't see a way. Remember how He gave you peace when it made no sense for you to have peace. Remember how He gave you strength to do what you couldn't do on your own. Those victories in your past become fuel for your faith. You'll know He did it for you back then, so He'll do it for you again.

Every victory is not just for the present time. You'll need those victories to encourage you in your future. If you shrink back in fear and play it safe all the time, you're not going to have what you need for where God is taking you.

God doesn't send trouble, but He allows things to happen so we can grow. We may not understand it, but I have never come out of a hard season where I wasn't better. When it was all said and done, I look back and can see how that challenge made me stronger, that situation made me wiser, that obstacle made me more confident. It gave me a greater trust in God and put me closer to my destiny.

The Scripture says God takes us from glory to glory (see 2 Corinthians 3:18). He takes us from victory to victory. That last victory you had — you're going to need it for the next victory.

Maybe you've passed up opportunities. You think you've missed your chance. Trust me, you haven't. God is about to fuel your faith. This is your time. This is your moment. Your destiny is calling. Step into the scary place — that's where God is; that's where you'll see His favor. Greatness is waiting for you.

Those victories in your past become fuel for your faith. You'll know He did it for you back then, so He'll do it for you again.

Say "no more" to fear:

▶ **REFLECTION**

When Moses led the children of Israel out of Egypt, he said, *"This is a day to remember forever — the day of leaving Egypt and your slavery; for the Lord has brought you out with mighty miracles . . ."* (Exodus 13:3, TLB). Remember this day forever. Remember what God has done for you. Celebrate this day every year, and tell your children all that God has done. Repeatedly during the next 40 years of wandering, the Israelites were called upon to remember. Every time they remembered that day when God brought them out of Egypt, it fueled their faith. The answer to our fears, doubts, anger, and uncertainty is always the same: Remember.

_____

_____

_____

_____

_____

_____

_____

_____

_____

_____

_____

_____

_____

_____

Start living in faith:

▶ **APPLICATION**

Are you in a hard season? Is your faith burning out? When a fire burns out, what do you do? You add fuel — gasoline, firewood, oxygen — and it burns bright once again. Think of remembering as the fuel to your faith. Take some time to remember what God has done for you in the past, rehearse it over and over in your mind, and trust that He will show out for you again.

▶ **DECLARATION**

This is my time. This is my moment. He takes me from victory to victory. I trust His ways. I trust His timing. My faith is strong. I will not give up!

▶ **PRAYER**

God, use this season to fuel my faith. Use this situation to make me stronger, wiser, and more confident in who You are and where You are calling me. From glory to glory, Amen.

CHAPTER 5

Destiny Moments

First Kings 19 tells the story of a man named Elisha, who was minding his own business, plowing in his family's field, when the prophet Elijah came by. Following God's instructions, Elijah threw his mantle on Elisha, anointing him as his successor. God was calling Elisha to follow Elijah.

Some opportunities don't come a second time. They are destiny moments when it's either "now" or "never." This was one of those moments for Elisha. He had to choose between the life he knew with his family or step into the unknown and follow the prophet Elijah. Down in his spirit something said, "This is your destiny. This is your moment. Have faith. It's now or never." Elisha made his choice. He cut up the plow and

God didn't call us to be comfortable. He called us to take new ground, to advance the Kingdom.

burned it. He killed the ox and boiled the meat. He walked away from the familiar and into his destiny.

Life is too short to settle for things that you know are less than what is in you. The reason some people aren't happy is because they are bored. They have so much more in them, but they are stuck doing something mediocre. If that's where you are, look for new opportunities. Stretch, grow, take courses, learn, do your part, and God is going to send Elijah by. He'll bring you an opportunity that not only scares you but excites you. You'll know it's your destiny. When you know God has put something in your heart, you can't get away from it. You wake up thinking about it. It excites your spirit. You know you have to take the risk.

"What if I try and it doesn't work out?" What if you try and it does? What if you don't try and miss your destiny? What if you get to Heaven and God says, "I created you to do all these amazing things; why did you let people talk you out of it? Why did you let thoughts convince you that you couldn't do it? Why did you let fear hold you back?" When we come to the end of life, nothing will be sadder than to look back and wonder what we could have become if we had just had the faith to take some risks.

God didn't call us to be comfortable. He called us to take new ground, to advance the Kingdom. There is potential in you waiting to be released: businesses, ministries, inventions, books, songs, movies, and more. Don't settle for less than what He put in you. If you weren't afraid, it wouldn't be your destiny. It's time to seize your destiny moments!

Say "no more" to fear:

▶ **REFLECTION**

The Scripture is full of destiny moments. When Ruth refused to leave Naomi, saying, "... *Where you go I will go, and where you stay I will stay. Your people will be my people and your God my God*" (Ruth 1:16, NIV), that was her destiny moment. When Mordecai asked Esther, "... *who can say but that God has brought you into the palace for just such a time as this?*" (Esther 4:14, TLB), that was her destiny moment. When Jesus called to Simon and Andrew, "... *Come, follow me! ...*" (Mark 1:17, TLB), that was their destiny moment. Have you ever had a destiny moment — a "now or never" opportunity — come your way?

_____

_____

_____

_____

_____

_____

_____

_____

_____

_____

_____

_____

_____

_____

Start living in faith:

▶ **APPLICATION**

Are you living up to your full potential? If you're not challenged by your job, if you're not encouraged by the people in your life, if you don't enjoy how you spend your time, let God take you higher. Look for new opportunities. Pray for bigger dreams. Take the leap of faith that propels you into greatness.

▶ **DECLARATION**

There is more in me. I will not settle for less than all that God has for me. It's now or never. I am taking new ground. I am advancing the Kingdom. I am saying yes to my destiny.

▶ **PRAYER**

God, here I am; send me. I am ready to do more for You. I am ready to follow You into the unknown. You have placed a dream in my heart, and I am willing to take the next step even if I have to do it afraid. In Jesus' name, Amen.

CHAPTER 6

The Divine Architect

When an architect designs a building, he doesn't just design the outside — what it's going to look like, the color, the style, and the shape. He also designs the inner structure. He calculates all the loads that the building must bear — how much each floor will weigh; how much wind it will face; how much equipment, furniture, and the number of people who will be on it. Then he'll know how many steel beams he'll need, how deep to dig the piers, how thick to pour the foundation, and if any special reinforcements are required.

In California, buildings are designed to withstand earthquakes. In Florida, they are designed to withstand hurricanes. In Colorado, the weight of heavy snowfall is taken into consideration. It's all calculated ahead of time, before a single hammer is lifted. An architect doesn't wait until the middle of a storm to decide how many load-bearing walls he needs. The specs have been studied, calculated, and approved before construction ever begins.

In the same way, before you were born, before you showed up on planet Earth, your specs were carefully designed. God, the Divine Architect, strategically and precisely put in you exactly what you would need for every storm that you will face. He not only designed planets and solar systems, He designed you.

"For you created my inmost being; you knit me together in my mother's womb. I praise you because I am fearfully and wonderfully made; your works are wonderful, I know that full well. My frame was not hidden from you when I was made in the secret place, when I was woven together in the depths of the earth. Your eyes saw my unformed body; all the days ordained for me were written in your book before one of them came to be" (Psalm 139:13–16, NIV).

Before you were ever born, God designed your looks, your personality, your talents, as well as your infrastructure and the things that you cannot see. He planned ahead of time what strength, what boldness, what determination, what faith you would need for the challenges and obstacles ahead. He put in you the strength, the endurance, the fortitude, and the tenacity so that no matter what comes against you, it will not be too much to bear. He intentionally designed you for the life that you would live.

God designed you with exactly what you need. You may not be able to see it, but your beams are big enough, your walls are strong enough, your foundation is sure enough, and you can bear whatever comes your way.

Your eyes saw my unformed body; all the days ordained for me were written in your book before one of them came to be.

PSALM 139:16 (NIV)

Say "no more" to fear:

In the Book of Matthew, Jesus tells the story of two builders: one who built his house upon the rock and one who built his house upon the sand (see Matthew 7:24–27). When the rainy season came with torrential downpours, floods, and strong winds, what do you think happened? The house built upon the rock stood firm, but the house built upon the sand was washed away. God, the Divine Architect, designed you with everything you need to succeed in life. He designed you to withstand every storm. He would never be so foolish as to give you a shoddy foundation. Your life is built upon the Rock.

_____

_____

_____

_____

_____

_____

_____

_____

_____

_____

_____

_____

_____

Start living in faith:

▶ **APPLICATION**

Imagine God weaving you together in your mother's womb. What ingredients does He include to make you unique? How does it feel to think that He knows you so intimately and created you so intentionally, that nothing you are going through is a surprise to Him?

▶ **DECLARATION**

The Most High God, the Divine Architect, has given me everything I need to face this pressure. I've got what it takes. I'm strong enough. I'm determined enough. I'm bold enough. I am well able.

▶ **PRAYER**

God, I will not live in fear. You did not miscalculate when You created me. I believe You took into careful consideration all that I would need to succeed in life and designed me accordingly. My trust is in You — my firm Rock and my Redeemer. In Jesus' name, Amen.

CHAPTER 7

Until Pressure Comes

S ometimes you don't know what you can handle until you are forced to handle it. Until pressure comes, you don't know what is in you. If you are tempted to feel overwhelmed, it is because you don't realize what is in you. You haven't had to use all of your resources yet. But it's not a surprise to God. He knew ahead of time; that's why He made you so strong. He took into account opposition that you never knew you would encounter, trials you never knew you would face, setbacks that you never saw coming.

Paul said in 1 Corinthians 10:13 (ESV), "... *God is faithful, and he will not let you be tempted beyond your ability, but with the temptation he will also provide the way of escape, that you may be able to endure it.*" Paul was saying, God will never let you face more pressure than He has designed you to withstand. He would not be a just God if He knew you were going to encounter something but didn't give you the strength to endure it. He would never give you less than you need to succeed, because He is faithful.

When something happens that we've never faced — a loss, a setback, a disappointment — it's tempting to think, "I can't handle this. It's too overwhelming. It's going to sink me." The truth is, you wouldn't be facing it unless you could handle it. If it was too much to bear, God wouldn't have allowed it. The very fact that it happened is a sign that you are well able.

God didn't miscalculate when He created you. He didn't accidentally give you less strength than the load you would be required to bear. He didn't forget about the environment you would be in and the conditions you would come up against. When God laid out the plan for your life, He took into account every hurt, every injustice, every loss, and every mistake you would make; and He created you accordingly.

Nothing you face will cause you to collapse under the weight of it. Now, you can choose to collapse in your mind. You can give up and think, "I'm overwhelmed. Life is too much. The temptation is too strong." That's why the Scripture tells us in Hebrews 12:3 (KJV), not to ". . . *faint in your minds.*" Your spirit is strong enough — now get your mind strong enough.

Within you is everything you need to withstand the trials, outlast the opposition, overcome the injustice, and endure until the dream comes to pass. Do not give in to fear. You were made for this.

. . . God is faithful, and he will not let you be tempted beyond your ability, but with the temptation he will also provide the way of escape, that you may be able to endure it.

1 CORINTHIANS 10:13 (ESV)

Say "no more" to fear:

▶ **REFLECTION**

When Joseph was 17, he had dreams that his brothers would bow down and serve him (see Genesis 37). What he didn't know then was all that he would have to endure before the day would come . . . being thrown into a pit and left for dead, sold into slavery, accused of rape, falsely imprisoned. With each trial, he must have felt overwhelmed, wondering why God had given him those dreams. But no matter how difficult the circumstance, Joseph remained faithful. Every time, he came out stronger. Every time, God showed him the way out. Every time, God worked good out of it and led him to his destiny.

Start living in faith:

▶ **APPLICATION**

Do you trust God? Do you trust His Word when it says that with every temptation, He will give you a way out? And with each trial, He will be with you. If you are struggling with this, take a moment to share that with God and receive His peace and assuring presence that He is with you and for you.

▶ **DECLARATION**

I can do all things through Christ. I've been armed with strength for this battle. I may walk through the valley of the shadow of death, but I know a secret: I'm not staying here. This valley is not my home. I'm coming out better, stronger, victorious, into new levels of my destiny. God is working this out for my good.

▶ **PRAYER**

God, thank You for designing me to handle the pressures of life. Thank You that I am well able. Thank You for giving me strength and grace when I need it. Great is Thy faithfulness! In Jesus' name, Amen.

CHAPTER 8

Strong In The Lord

The apostle Paul had all kinds of unfair things happen to him. Three times he was beaten with rods. He was put in prison without a trial. He was shipwrecked and bitten by a poisonous snake. He could have collapsed under the pressure. Yet, he's the one who said, *"Now thanks be to God who always leads us in triumph . . ."* (2 Corinthians 2:14, NKJV).

Paul understood that God doesn't let you face things that you can't handle. The enemy didn't finally come up with a scheme to outwit the God who created you. If, like Paul, you'll stay in faith, you'll discover that God is leading you to victory.

On the way to your destiny there will be opposition, things that are not fair, and people who should be for you but turn against you. You don't have to get revenge. You don't have to live bitter. You can forgive and move forward.

Jesus said, in the Sermon on the Mount, *"Happy are those who are persecuted because they are good, for the Kingdom of Heaven is theirs. When you are reviled and persecuted and lied about because you are my followers — wonderful!"* (Matthew 5:10–11, TLB). Happy?! Wonderful?! What is so wonderful about being wrongfully accused, lied about, bullied, shamed, and persecuted? The answer is in the next verse: *". . . a tremendous reward awaits you . . ."* (v. 12, TLB). When you stay in faith, you'll discover your reward. You'll discover that God is leading you to victory.

Maybe you're in a test now. You think it's too much to bear. "These people at work are not fair; this situation with my child has me overwhelmed; this illness I'm dealing with is stressing me out." Have a new perspective: God always causes us to triumph; great is thy reward!

In Isaiah 27:5 (NKJV), God says, *". . . take hold of My strength. . . ."* Instead of thinking about how difficult your situation is, take hold of God's strength. Lean on Him as you focus on your reward.

It will be overwhelming if you don't remind yourself that whatever you are going through is not a surprise to God. Paul said in 2 Corinthians 4:8 (NIV), *"We are hard pressed on every side, but not crushed. . . ."* He was saying, in effect, we were designed for this. When you face a big challenge, it's because God has equipped you to handle it — not on your own, but by taking hold of His strength as you move forward.

Instead of thinking about how difficult your situation is, take hold of God's strength. Lean on Him as you focus on your reward.

Say "no more" to fear:

▶ **REFLECTION**

First Samuel tells the story of Elkanah who had two wives: Hannah and Peninnah. Peninnah had children, but Hannah had none. What made matters worse, Peninnah constantly teased Hannah about her barrenness. She wanted Hannah to feel miserable and took every opportunity to rub it in her face. Talk about unfair! But Hannah had something that Peninnah clearly did not — a relationship with the Lord. Hannah turned to God for His strength. She stayed in faith, and baby Samuel was her reward.

Start living in faith:

▶ **APPLICATION**

Have you every been lied about or falsely accused, and God asked you to keep your mouth shut — to turn the other cheek rather than defend yourself? The next time you feel words of retaliation rise up, bite your tongue and remember: The Lord is your strength; a tremendous reward awaits you!

▶ **DECLARATION**

The Kingdom of Heaven is my reward. God is leading me to victory. He is my strength and my portion. I will not be crushed. With God by my side, I cannot fail.

▶ **PRAYER**

God, I need You. I need Your strength. Help me so that I do not give voice to my fears and doubts when life gets hard. Take my hand and lead me to victory! In Jesus' name, Amen.

CHAPTER 9

Made For More

When we acquired the Compaq Center as our central campus, we knew it would require some renovation to meet our needs. It was built as a sports arena, but we needed classrooms, a youth facility, a chapel, and offices. We told the architects one day we wanted to add a five-story building that attached to the lobbies. They designed the infrastructure — the foundation, beams, and piers — to accommodate ten stories.

When you look at the outside, you see a five-story building. What you can't see, unless you get the architect's plans, is that it's designed for ten stories. People driving down the freeway think: *That building is finished; it's as tall as it will ever be.* They don't know what's underground. What makes

The path of the righteous is like the morning sun, shining ever brighter till the full light of day.

PROVERBS 4:18 (NIV)

it capable of going up higher is not what is on the outside; it's the weight the infrastructure was designed to hold.

You may think you've reached your limits. You've been at a certain level for a long time. Can I encourage you . . . you have more floors in you! You've done well with the pressure you have faced. You've gotten comfortable carrying this load. But if you could look at your specs, if you could see the plans God has for you, you would notice your beams are much bigger than what you're carrying right now.

Proverbs 4:18 (NIV) says, *"The path of the righteous is like the morning sun, shining ever brighter till the full light of day."* Where you are is not your final destination. God's plan for you is about to get brighter and brighter.

God wants to increase your capacity because you have been designed for more. You could think God overdesigned you, but He doesn't put anything in you that you don't need. God has new levels for you. With increase comes a pressure that will make you stretch, grow, and release your faith. With increase you will believe bigger, dream bigger, and take on new challenges. You'll discover you were designed to handle so much more — things that you didn't think you could handle.

Some of the things that overwhelmed you ten years ago, you can look back now and say, "It's no big deal. I thought that trouble at work was going to give me a nervous breakdown, but I've come through it, and now things like that don't bother me." It's not so much that God changed the circumstances; it's that God changed you. He showed you who you really are. Now when new challenges come, you don't have to let it overwhelm you. You can let it inspire you. You know you're going to discover abilities that you didn't know you had. Don't complain about the difficult times; that's when you discover there's more in you.

Say "no more" to fear:

▶ **REFLECTION**

When we first meet the apostle Paul in Scripture, he goes by the name Saul and is famous for persecuting Christians. When we first meet Simon Peter, he is a fisherman. When we first meet Mary, she is a newly engaged teenager. In each case, God had so much more planned for their lives. Paul went on to write the majority of the New Testament. Peter led 3,000 people to Christ in one day. Mary gave birth to Jesus. Just like Paul, Simon Peter, and Mary, you have more in you than you can see right now. Do you sense where God might be taking you?

_____

_____

_____

_____

_____

_____

_____

_____

_____

_____

_____

_____

_____

Start living in faith:

▶ **APPLICATION**

What is the hardest thing you have ever gone through? How did God change you through that experience? Thank Him for the ways He strengthened you in that difficulty and revealed to you a strength you never knew was in you.

▶ **DECLARATION**

God is taking me to new heights. His plan for me keeps getting brighter and brighter. This is not my final destination. I am capable of more. I was made for more.

▶ **PRAYER**

God, Your Word says that Your plans for me are beyond my wildest imagination. Put the dream You have for me in my heart so I can reach for new heights. I am ready to take this to the next level. I will step into your promise. In Jesus' name, Amen.

CHAPTER 10

Faith In
The Right
Direction

Fear and faith have something in common. They both ask us to believe something is going to happen that we cannot see.

Fear says, "That pain in your side — that's the same thing that your grandmother died from. It will probably be the end of you." Faith says, "That sickness is not permanent. It's only temporary." Fear says, "Business is slow. You're going to go under." Faith says, "God is supplying all of your needs." Fear says, "You've been through so much. You're never going to be happy." Faith says, "Your best days are still ahead."

If you go around all day playing your fears over and over in your mind, you allow that to become a reality. That's what Job was saying when he lamented, *"What I feared has come upon me; what I dreaded has happened to me"* (Job 3:25, NIV). Really, fear is just using your faith in the wrong direction. Your faith will work in the negative as well as the positive.

Years ago I was facing a situation that had the potential to turn out really badly. It had been going on for months. Every morning when I woke up, the first thought that came to my mind was, "It's not going to work out. It's going to cause all kinds of heartache." That's the way fear is; it will try to dominate your thoughts. If you allow it, fear will keep you awake at night.

I was so tempted to worry and go around all stressed out. But one day, I heard God say something to me. Not out loud, but right down in my spirit. He said, "Joel, if you keep worrying and going over all the reasons why it's not going to work out, then because of your worry, you're going to allow it to come to pass. But if you will trust Me and use that same energy to believe, I will turn it around and cause it to work out to your advantage." When I heard that, I got a new perspective. I realized that having worry, fear, and negative thoughts is not just a bad habit; it's faith in the wrong direction, and it gives the negative the right to come to pass.

Just as faith can bring in good things, fear can bring in negative things. When you go around worried and expecting the worst, it's like you're inviting that into your life. Quit inviting defeat, sickness, and bad breaks by using your faith in the wrong direction. Start inviting victory. Start thinking and speaking the positive. Use your faith in the right direction.

Fear and faith have something in common. They both ask us to believe something is going to happen that we cannot see.

Say "no more" to fear:

Every night for years and years, a woman thought she heard a burglar downstairs. She would make her husband get up at least once a week during the night to check and make sure the doors were locked and that no one had broken in. One night, the husband was surprised to find himself face-to-face with an armed robber. The man said he didn't want to hurt him; he just wanted all his valuables. The husband said, "Before you go, will you come up and meet my wife? She's been waiting 30 years to meet you." If you go through life expecting disaster, you are putting your faith in your fears, and you will lose a lot of unnecessary sleep over it.

_____

_____

_____

_____

_____

_____

_____

_____

_____

_____

_____

_____

Start living in faith:

▶ **APPLICATION**

What are you worried about? Are you always waiting for "the other shoe to drop"? When fear rises up, telling you that something bad is going to happen, turn your faith in the right direction. Believe that God has a good plan for your life and that He will cause all things to work out for your good.

▶ **DECLARATION**

I choose to put my faith in God, not my fears. Everything I put my hand to will prosper. God's hedge of protection is around me and my family. I will not fear, for God is always with me.

▶ **PRAYER**

God, I want my mind to be filled with thoughts of You. I want to have faith in the right direction . . . faith for the good and perfect and pleasing will You have for my life. With You by my side, I will not give in to fear. In Jesus' name, Amen.

CHAPTER 11

Get In Agreement

When our son Jonathan was a little baby, Victoria and I took him with us one evening to a restaurant. As we were eating dinner, an older couple came up and complimented us on what a good baby he was being. They were very friendly, but just before they left, the man turned around and said, "Wait until he gets to be about two years old. It's like they turn into another person. He's good now, but those terrible twos are coming."

I wanted to say, "Thank you so much for your encouragement. You really lifted my spirits." Instead I told Victoria, "I don't receive that. I don't agree with that. I'm not letting that take root. It's not going to be the terrible twos for us; it's going to be the terrific twos." And do you know, we never had a problem with him in his twos or threes or fours.

Before we knew it, Jonathan was 10 years old. He was still a great kid, but people started saying, "Just wait till he gets to be a teenager." Next people will say, "Just wait till he gets to be 21." And then they'll say, "Wait till he hits 40 and has a mid-life crisis." And "Wait till he's 75."

The Scripture says that if any two of you agree, it shall be done (Matthew 18:19–20). It's a promise that, when we stand in faith with another believer, God will do what He said. I believe the same principle is true in the negative. If the enemy puts a thought in your mind and you agree, then your agreement is what gives it the power to come to pass. But if you don't agree, you turn it around.

The thought comes, "Your child is going to get into trouble." No, I don't agree. My children will be mighty in the land. My children will fulfill their destiny.

The thought comes, "You better not go out today. You're going to get in an accident." No, I don't agree. God has a hedge of protection around me — a blood line the enemy cannot cross.

The thought comes, "You're going to die from that same sickness your grandmother had. You might as well get ready. It's been in your family line for three generations." No, I don't agree. With long life God will satisfy me. My body is a temple of the Most High God. Sickness cannot live in me.

The key is, don't come into agreement with negative, discouraging thoughts. Don't agree with defeat, mediocrity, trouble, or disappointments. Pay attention to what you're agreeing with. Agree with what God says, and it will come to pass.

Pay attention to what you're agreeing with. Agree with what God says, and it will come to pass.

Say "no more" to fear:

▶ **REFLECTION**

In Matthew 18, Jesus says that if any two agree on something, God will do it. The Amplified version says that if two of you ". . . *make a symphony together . . . it will come to pass . . .*" (v. 19, AMPC). When you think about agreeing with someone as making music with them, it offers an interesting picture. A symphony is only beautiful when everyone is playing the right notes. As soon as someone hits a wrong note — a flat that should have been a sharp, an A that should have been an E minor — everyone cringes. But when you get in agreement with the right notes, the right thoughts, the right attitudes, you are making a joyful noise unto the Lord. When you agree with God, you make beautiful music!

Start living in faith:

▶ **APPLICATION**

Jesus tells us to love our enemies, but He doesn't tell us we have to agree with them. When the enemy puts negative, discouraging thoughts in your mind, you can say, "I disagree with you. Good is coming my way." You have the choice: to agree with the enemy or to agree with God.

▶ **DECLARATION**

I am in the world but not of the world. My mind is being transformed by the Word of God and the promises God has for my life. No weapon formed against me will prosper. I choose to agree with God and receive His blessings for my life.

▶ **PRAYER**

God, You promised that where two agree, it will be done. You said You have a good plan for my life; I come into agreement with You. You said nothing will separate me from Your love; I come into fellowship with You. I believe that You are with me, working all things together for my good. In Jesus' name, Amen.

CHAPTER 12

A Disciplined Mind

I read about a woman who bought a six-foot ficus tree for her bedroom. She was very experienced with plants. She had them all over her house. One morning, she got up and looked at that tree, and when the thought came to her, thought, "That plant is not going to make it. It's going to die." The tree was healthy. There was not a thing wrong with it. But she made the mistake of believing that thought. She even told her husband, "I'm afraid this plant is not going to make it. I think I wasted my money." He said, "What are you talking about? It's perfectly healthy. All of our other plants are doing just fine."

Three weeks later, she got up, and every leaf on that tree had turned yellow. A couple days later, all the leaves had fallen off. A few days after that, the whole tree had withered up and died.

For God has not given us a spirit of fear, but of power and of love and of a sound mind.

2 TIMOTHY 1:7 (NKJV)

Later, as the woman was praying, she heard God say to her, "You killed that plant with your thoughts." She said to her husband, "I know this sounds totally crazy, but I think I killed that plant with my thoughts." He looked at her strangely and said, "All I can say is, I hope you're thinking good thoughts about me."

I wonder how many of our dreams we have killed with our thoughts. How many times have we stopped God's blessings because we were dwelling on fear, doubt, and negativity? If we are not disciplined in our thought life, the nagging feeling that things aren't going to turn out will start to take root.

Second Timothy 1:7 (NKJV) says, *"For God has not given us a spirit of fear, but of power and of love and of a sound mind."* The Amplified version says a "disciplined" mind. In other words, we're not going to overcome fear and live a powerful, victorious life if we're not disciplined in our thought life. That's where the real battle is taking place.

On my father's side of the family, there is a long line of heart disease. My grandfather died early from heart disease. Many of my dad's brothers and other family members died early deaths as well. It would be easy for me to give into that fear and think, "It's just a matter of time before it happens to me." But I don't accept that. I've learned to be disciplined in my thoughts. I'm not inviting sickness into my life.

Your mind is the enemy's bull's-eye. If he can control your thoughts, he can control your life. If you don't guard your mind, it will default back to thoughts of fear, worry, defeat, failure, and negativity. You have to stay disciplined in your thought life. Your thoughts are very powerful.

Say "no more" to fear:

▶ **REFLECTION**

My grandmother on my father's side was a very feisty woman. She reminded me of Granny on *The Beverly Hillbillies*. She was one of a kind. Later in life, she went to the doctor. He said, "I'm sorry, Mrs. Osteen, but you have the beginning stages of Parkinson's disease." That did not set well with Grandmother Osteen. She said, "Listen here, Doctor. I will not have it. I refuse to have it. I'm too old to have it." She went home, and what do you know, she never did develop Parkinson's disease. She lived out her days in good health. We can't always just wish things away, but we can discipline our minds to choose faith instead of fear, activating God's power in our lives.

Start living in faith:

▶ **APPLICATION**

Have you ever dismissed one of your dreams with your thoughts? Have you ever reasoned your way out of a blessing? Find a scripture that speaks to you, that tells of the promises God has for your life. Repeat it over and over throughout your day as you discipline your mind to believe the best. Then, when an opportunity comes, you can respond with faith instead of fear.

▶ **DECLARATION**

I trust God. I delight in His promises, both day and night. My life bears fruit. Everything I touch prospers. My days are full of joy. He strengthens me in times of trouble and works all things together for my good.

▶ **PRAYER**

God, thank You for giving me a spirit of power. Thank You for giving me a spirit of love. Thank You for giving me a disciplined mind. Your favor is for a lifetime. With You leading me, I will live a victorious life. In Jesus' name, Amen.

CHAPTER 13

Tearing Down Strongholds

One Sunday, I spoke to a young couple after the service here at Lakewood. They were very discouraged. They had been trying to have a child for many years, but the young lady wasn't able to conceive.

They had been to several doctors, and everything seemed to be fine, so they couldn't understand why she couldn't get pregnant.

The woman was very frustrated when she told me, "Joel, my mother had a terrible time conceiving. My grandmother had the same problem. From the time I was a little girl, I've always been afraid that I wouldn't be able to have a child."

"Always" . . . "From the time I was a little girl" . . . these were clues to me that fear had created a stronghold in her mind. The first place we lose the victory is in our own thinking. The good news is, you can change your mind. You can change what you're in agreement with. Instead of activating your fear, you can activate your faith.

Second Corinthians 10:4 (NIV) says, *"The weapons we fight with are not the weapons of the world. On the contrary, they have divine power to demolish strongholds."* Another version calls them *"strongholds of human reasoning"* and *"false arguments"* (NLT). When fear gets a hold of your thoughts, it will lie to you and try to talk you out of your destiny. That's when you know it's time to trade your fear for faith.

I told this young woman that, instead of worrying and thinking she would never get pregnant, she had to start meditating on what God says. All through the day, I said, rehearse God's promises for your life: "Father, You said the fruit of my womb is blessed. Children are a gift from God. No good thing will God withhold because I walk uprightly. Lord, thank You that I am able to conceive." She followed my advice and started activating her faith. Slowly, God's promises chipped away at the stronghold in her mind.

About a year later, I saw this couple in the lobby. They were beaming with joy. They were pregnant with a baby boy. Today, that child is healthy and whole. I don't know if that would have happened if she had not changed what she was meditating on.

Throughout life, fear will come knocking at your door. Fear will tell you all the worst-case scenarios, trying to create a stronghold in your mind. Here's a key: When fear knocks, let faith answer the door. Use the divine power within you to slam the door on negative thinking. Don't give those thoughts the time of day. Answer back with faith.

*The weapons we fight with are
not the weapons of the world.
On the contrary, they have divine
power to demolish strongholds.*
2 CORINTHIANS 10:4 (NIV)

Say "no more" to fear:

When God called out to Moses from the burning bush and told him to go to Egypt to rescue the Israelites, Moses was full of excuses. One of those excuses was, "... *I'm not very good with words. I never have been, and I'm not now, even though you have spoken to me. I get tongue-tied, and my words get tangled*" (Exodus 4:10, NLT). Clearly, Moses had let his speech impediment become a stronghold in his mind. He didn't believe God could ever use him in a mighty way because of it. Even though God promised him it would all work out, Moses had a hard time believing. Don't let your fears take root. Remove them out of your thoughts before they can take hold of your mind and prevent you from reaching your destiny.

Start living in faith:

▶ **APPLICATION**

Have you ever felt like something had a stronghold on your mind? No matter what you did, no matter how good life was, that nagging feeling was always there telling you it would never work out. It is time to pull down strongholds by thinking on and receiving God's goodness and promises.

▶ **DECLARATION**

The strongholds in my mind can no longer lie to me. I choose to rely on God's almighty power at work within me. I am clothed with the belt of truth, the breastplate of righteousness, the Gospel of peace, the shield of faith, the helmet of salvation, and the Word of God. Fear doesn't stand a chance.

▶ **PRAYER**

God, when fear comes knocking, help me answer with faith. Generational curses are broken with me. Strongholds are broken in me. It's time for a new beginning. In Jesus' name, Amen.

CHAPTER 14

Fear Like A Fog

Once, when I was flying out of Canada, our flight was delayed because of fog. We could barely see. It seemed like the whole city was covered. When the plane eventually took off, we didn't have to go far to get above the fog. Looking down, we could see that it was just a small pocket of dense fog, covering about a one-mile area around the airport.

That's the way fear is — it presents itself much bigger than it really is. Fear will tell you how bad, how long, and how hard something is going to be.

Fear will tell you that pain in your side is terminal when really, you just shouldn't have had that last piece of pizza.

Fear will tell you your happiness will never last, but the Bible says that God's favor is not for a season; it's for a lifetime.

When fear tries to make you panic, just smile and say, "Fear, I know your tricks. You're all bark and no bite. You look big, but I'm not impressed. I know there is nothing to you."

When you activate faith, the greatest force in the universe goes to work. Those problems may look big, but our God is bigger. The obstacles may look high, but our God is the Most High. When thoughts of fear, worry, and doubt come, you've got to say like King David, *"The Lord is my light and my salvation — so why should I be afraid? The Lord is my fortress, protecting me from danger, so why should I tremble? When evil people come to devour me, when my enemies and foes attack me, they will stumble and fall. Though a mighty army surrounds me, my heart will not be afraid. Even if I am attacked, I will remain confident"* (Psalm 27:1–3, NLT).

In other words, "I will not fear. I will not worry. I will not live discouraged. I will not be defeated. I will not dwell on the negative. I know who I am, and I know whose I am. I may feel trapped, I may not see a way out, the medical report doesn't look good, my bank statement says I'm not going to make it, but I know a secret: The Lord is my strength, and He is on my side."

Think about this: If the thing you fear can come upon you, how much more can the things you have *faith* for come upon you? Friends, your destiny is too great, your assignment is too important, and your time is too valuable to give into fear. Do not let fear intimidate you. You are a child of the Most High God.

When you activate faith, the greatest force in the universe goes to work. Those problems may look big, but our God is bigger.

Say "no more" to fear:

▶ **REFLECTION**

James 4:14 says that the morning fog is "... *here a little while, then it's gone*" (NLT). Now you see it, now you don't. He was comparing the fog to our lives — tomorrow isn't promised, but if it does come, we can't predict what it will bring with it. When you give too much weight to the fear — to the fog — you are wasting your time. Only God knows what tomorrow will bring. Trust that He sees the bigger picture. He is working all things together for your good. His grace and mercy and love are not fleeting like the morning fog, but rather they endure for a lifetime.

Start living in faith:

Have you ever felt like your mind was in a fog — that you just weren't thinking clearly? When you let the enemy control your thoughts, it's like trying to navigate life in a fog. The enemy will try to convince you that the fog will never clear, but the fog isn't as dense as it looks. The answer is right around the corner. Clarity will come by spending time in prayer and reading God's Word.

▶ **DECLARATION**

The enemy doesn't have the final say; God has the final say. The fog will clear. I will overcome every obstacle. I will defeat every enemy. I will become everything He has created me to be because I am a child of the Most High God.

▶ **PRAYER**

God, You are a light to the world and a lamp to my feet. Protect me from my enemies. Lead me and guide me all the days of my life. My confidence is in You. I will not be afraid. In Jesus' name, Amen.

CHAPTER 15

You Can Handle It

B ack in the 1950s, my father was pastoring a successful denominational church. His future looked bright. They had just built a beautiful new sanctuary. But through a series of events, he had to leave that church and start all over. It was a major setback. He'd given years of his life there. Daddy could have sat around nursing his wounds, feeling sorry for himself. Instead, his attitude was, "I can handle it." He knew when one door closes, God always opens another door. In fact, God uses closed doors as much as He uses open ones. After that door closed, my father and my mother started Lakewood, and here we are today still going strong.

Paul said in Philippians 4:13 (AMPC), *"I have strength for all things in Christ Who empowers me [I am ready for anything and equal to anything*

I have strength for all things in Christ Who empowers me [I am ready for anything and equal to anything through Him Who infuses inner strength into me; I am self-sufficient in Christ's sufficiency].

PHILIPPIANS 4:13 (AMPC)

through Him Who infuses inner strength into me; I am self-sufficient in Christ's sufficiency]." Listen to his confession: I am ready for and equal to anything. He was saying, "The enemy can hit me with his best shot, but it's not going to stop me. I am more than a conqueror."

Paul had been through a shipwreck, spent the night on the open sea, and went days without food. He was falsely accused, beaten with rods, and put in prison. If anybody had a reason to get discouraged, depressed, and bitter, it would have been him. But he understood this principle. His attitude was, "I can handle it. I'm ready for anything. I'm equal to anything. Why? Because Almighty God, the Creator of the universe, has infused His strength into me. He's equipped me, empowered me, anointed me, crowned me with favor, put royal blood in my veins, and called me to reign in life."

This is what Joseph did. He was betrayed by his brothers, thrown into a pit, and spent 13 years in prison for something he didn't do. He didn't get depressed. He didn't start complaining. He didn't blame God. His attitude was, "I can handle it. God is still on the throne. He wouldn't have allowed it unless He had a purpose, so I'm going to stay in faith and keep being my best." When it was all said and done, Joseph was second-in-command of all of Egypt.

No person can keep you from your destiny. No disappointment, no bad break, and no sickness can stop God's will for your life. You are full of can-do power. You can handle it! Start believing it for yourself.

Say "no more" to fear:

When Mary and Joseph took Jesus to the temple to be dedicated when he was eight days old, a widow named Anna was there. In fact, she'd been there for decades. Anna had been married for seven years, but when her husband died, she devoted herself to fasting and praying. Anna could have been bitter and resentful that her husband died so young, that she never married again, that she never had children, that she didn't have a place of her own. Instead, she believed that because God was with her, she could handle it, and her faithfulness was rewarded. She was one of the first people to lay eyes on the Christ child.

Start living in faith:

▶ **APPLICATION**

Anna was over 80 years old before she saw the promise and fulfillment in Jesus. What is the longest you have ever been required to wait for something? What are you currently waiting for? How long are you willing to wait for the promises of God to come to pass in your life? Remind yourself in the waiting: The promise is coming!

▶ **DECLARATION**

The same spirit that raised Christ from the dead lives in me. Therefore, I walk in victory, and I can handle it. My boss, my child, the health report, that family member — whatever comes my way, I can handle it!

▶ **PRAYER**

God, I trust You. I know that anything that I face today, I can handle because You are with me. If You are bringing me to it, then You will bring me through it. In fact, I'll come out stronger on the other side! In Jesus' name, Amen.

CHAPTER 16

Victor Mentality

I have a friend who has had cancer three times, yet I've never once heard him complain. I've never seen him depressed. For a long time, nobody even knew he was sick because he had such a great attitude. He lived with a victor mentality.

When the cancer came back for the third time, the doctors told him they were going to harvest his white blood cells so they could use them to help restore his immune system after the chemotherapy treatments. These are the killer cells that fight off cancer. My friend asked the doctors how many of these white blood cells they needed. They gave him a number. He said to the doctors, "I'll give you twice what you need."

For the next couple of months, all through the day, my friend prayed, "Father, thank You that my white blood cells are multiplying. They're getting stronger and more effective. They will do exactly what You created them to do." Two months later, he went back to the hospital. The doctor said, "You're a man of your word. You gave us more than twice what we were hoping for." He went through the treatment, and today my friend is cancer-free.

Philippians 1:28 (AMPC) says, *"And do not [for a moment] be frightened or intimidated in anything by your opponents and adversaries, for such [constancy and fearlessness] will be a clear sign (proof and seal) to them of [their impending] destruction, but [a sure token and evidence] of your deliverance and salvation, and that from God."*

Don't be intimidated by your opponents. They're no match for you. Don't be intimidated by that financial problem, what somebody said about you, that situation at work, that cancer. There is an anointing on your life that seals you, protects you, empowers you, and enables you. You've been infused with strength. When you have this victor mentality — this attitude of faith — knowing that you're equipped and empowered with God's strength, then all the forces of darkness cannot defeat you.

The Scripture says, *". . . let the weak say, I am strong"* (Joel 3:10, KJV). If you're always talking about the problem, all that's doing is making you weaker. When you talk defeat, strength is leaving, energy is leaving, and creativity is leaving. Quit letting those things overwhelm you. You are not a victim; you are a victor. If it came your way, you can handle it. You're ready for it. You're equal to it. That difficulty won't defeat you; it will promote you. Fearlessness is a clear sign of victory!

There is an anointing on your life that seals you, protects you, empowers you, and enables you. You've been infused with strength.

Say "no more" to fear:

Moses sent twelve men to spy out the Promised Land (see Numbers 13). Ten of them came back with negative reports: *The people there are bigger, stronger, and more powerful than us; we'll never be able to defeat them.* They had a victim mentality. But two men, Joshua and Caleb, came back ready to fight. ". . . *We should go up and take possession of the land, for we can certainly do it,*" Caleb said (Numbers 13:30, NIV). He and Joshua had a victor mentality. They knew that with God on their side, the other armies didn't stand a chance. When you are up against something that is bigger than you, or that is outside of your experience or expectations, do you rise up with a victor mentality and enter the Promised Land, or do you shrink in fear?

Start living in faith:

▶ **APPLICATION**

Are you currently facing a huge challenge? If you're not now, fasten your seatbelt. It's right around the corner! Whatever the situation is, you can rise up and take your Promised Land. Quit talking about your problems, and start talking about God's promises. Rehearse them over and over until you see victory come to pass in your life.

▶ **DECLARATION**

I'm a victor, not a victim. The most powerful force in the universe is on my side. I am equipped and empowered with God's strength. I will not bow down to fear. I will stand up and fight. Victory is mine!

▶ **PRAYER**

God, thank You for always being by my side. Thank You for being my strength when I am weak. Thank You for giving me victory when it looks impossible. Thank You for preparing the path to my Promised Land. In Jesus' name, Amen.

CHAPTER 17

Still Standing

I heard a story about a wealthy man who was known for being eccentric. One day, he threw a backyard party and filled his swimming pool with sharks and alligators. He announced to his guests, "Anyone who will swim across my pool, I'll give you anything you want." In a few minutes, there was a big splash. A man swam frantically, dodging alligators, maneuvering around sharks, and made it to the other side just in the nick of time. The wealthy man went to him and said, "I can't believe it! You're the bravest man I've ever met. Now, what do you want?" The man said, "What I want more than anything is the name of the person who pushed me in."

Sometimes in life, we get pushed in. Things happen that we didn't see coming . . . a bad medical report, a relationship ends, a business goes under. Don't fall into self-pity. Do like the man in the pool — keep swimming. Keep moving forward, doing the right thing, and honoring God. He has already given you the strength, the wisdom, and the favor to not only make it through but to come out better.

Matthew 5:45 (NLT) says that God "*. . . sends rain on the just and the unjust alike.*" Being a person of faith doesn't exempt us from difficulties. The sun rises on the good and the bad; the rain pours down on the righteous and the not-so-righteous; the holy are just as likely to get pushed in as the unholy.

It's easy to think, "I honor God. I go to church. I'm good to people. So why do I have more problems than that person down the street who doesn't have anything to do with God?" Jesus told a parable about this. In the parable, one person built their house on the rock — they honored God. The other person built their house on the sand — they didn't honor God. What's interesting is, the storm came to both people. The wind and the rain fell on both houses. But after the storm, only one house was left standing.

When you honor God, the storms will still come. The difference is, when it's all said and done, you'll still be standing, while the other house will be washed away. The enemy may hit you with his best shot, but because your house is built on the rock, the enemy's best will never be enough. When the storm is over, you'll come out stronger. You'll find yourself better than you were before.

When the storm is over, you'll come out stronger. You'll find yourself better than you were before.

Say "no more" to fear:

In 1945, an atomic bomb was dropped on Nagasaki, Japan. Found in the rubble was a perfectly intact cross. In 2001, the World Trade Center collapsed when the Twin Towers were struck. Found at Ground Zero was a page from Scripture, fused to a piece of steel. You've probably heard of other disasters — house fires, tornadoes, floods — in which a Bible or cross or portrait of Jesus was all that survived. Storms will come, but God's plans and promises still stand.

_____

_____

_____

_____

_____

_____

_____

_____

_____

_____

_____

_____

_____

_____

_____

_____

Start living in faith:

▶ **APPLICATION**

Have you ever been in a situation that should have broken you, but you came out stronger on the other side? Have you ever had peace when everything was falling apart? If you've ever found yourself still standing in the midst of a storm, you know that it is because you have God in your life. Take time to thank Him for being your Rock and helping you weather the storm.

▶ **DECLARATION**

I am ready for anything. My life is rooted and grounded in the Word of God. He is the Rock of my salvation. No matter what comes against me, I'll still be here. I have faced storms before, and I'm still standing. This difficulty will not defeat me; it will promote me to the next level.

▶ **PRAYER**

God, help me weather this storm. I cling to You, knowing that You are making me stronger. Do not abandon me. I can't do this without You. Thank You that I don't have to. In Jesus' name, Amen.

CHAPTER 18

Trial By Fire

I once read about a businessman who worked in management for a large home improvement company that had retail stores all over the country. This gentleman was way up there in senior management. He'd been at the company for over 30 years. In fact, he had helped build the company from the ground up. One day, however, during corporate restructuring, the company decided that they no longer needed him.

When you face difficulties, you have to remind yourself: It may be unexpected to you, but it's not a surprise to God. It didn't catch Him off guard. He's not in the heavens scratching His head saying, "Oh no, he got laid off. That messed everything up! What am I going to do now?" God knows the end from the beginning. He's already written every day of your life in His Book. The good news is, if you'll stay in faith, your book will end in victory.

Instead of looking for another job, this businessman got a couple of his friends together, and they started their own company. They called it The Home Depot. You've no doubt heard of the largest and most successful home improvement store in the country.

What I am saying is that difficulty is not meant to defeat you; it's meant to promote you. A setback is simply a setup for a greater comeback.

"Oh, Joel, it's so hard. It was unfair. I don't understand it." That is talking yourself into defeat. If it was too much, God wouldn't have allowed it. Start talking to yourself in a new way: "I am well able. I'm equipped. I'm empowered. I'm ready for anything. God has something better in store for me."

The fact is, God is not going to deliver us from every difficulty. He's not going to keep us from every challenge. If He did, we would never grow.

It says in 1 Peter 1:7 (TLB), *"These trials are only to test your faith, to see whether or not it is strong and pure. It is being tested as fire tests gold and purifies it — and your faith is far more precious to God than mere gold; so if your faith remains strong after being tried in the test tube of fiery trials, it will bring you much praise and glory and honor on the day of his return."*

Faith is tried in the fire of affliction. When you're in a tough time, that's an opportunity to show the world what you're made of. Anybody can get negative, bitter, lose their passion, and blame God. That's easy. But if you want to pass the test, if you want God to take you to a new level, you will face the trial by fire head-on and come out stronger and more refined on the other side.

Faith is tried in the fire of affliction. When you're in a tough time, that's an opportunity to show the world what you're made of.

Say "no more" to fear:

Walt Disney was once fired from a job because he "lacked imagination." Oprah was fired from her job as a news reporter because she was too emotionally connected to her stories. Elvis Presley was told not to quit his day job (as a truck driver). Van Gogh only sold one painting in his lifetime. Michael Jordan was cut from his high school basketball team. Isaac Newton failed at running his family farm, so he took up mathematics. Thomas Edison was fired from Western Union and took up inventing. Each of these individuals has something in common: They didn't let the trials they faced break them. They took failure and rejection in stride and used it to catapult them into their destiny.

Start living in faith:

▶ **APPLICATION**

When was the last time you failed at something? When was the last time you were fired or rejected? How did you respond to that setback? Did it shake your faith? Or did it inspire you to try harder, to pursue a dream you had been putting off? The next time you face rejection, remember: Every setback has the potential to be a setup for greatness!

▶ **DECLARATION**

This is not the end. This is a new beginning. I am well able. I am equipped. I am empowered. I am ready for anything. God has something better in store for me. I am one step closer to my destiny.

▶ **PRAYER**

God, use this trial to move me toward my destiny. Use this test to refine my faith. Strengthen me so that when hard times come, my faith will not waiver. I give You all the praise and glory and honor. In Jesus' name, Amen.

CHAPTER 19

A Spider's Anointing

We've all seen how a spider spins its web in order to catch insects. The web is filled with a sticky substance. So when insects come into it, they not only get tangled in the web, they actually get stuck. That's why sometimes you'll see a big dragonfly in a small web. A little spider can capture insects 10 times its size, thanks to the web it spins.

Have you ever wondered how those insects get stuck, but the spider that made the web can walk across it without getting stuck? It seems like the spider would get caught in its own trap. God made the spider so that its body secretes special oil that flows down to its legs, making it possible for the spider to glide across the web. In other words, the spider doesn't get stuck because of the anointing that's on its life.

In the same way, God has put an anointing on your life. It's like oil that keeps things from sticking. When you walk in your anointing, knowing that you can handle anything that comes your way, then things that should bring you down won't. A relationship comes to an end. You should be bitter. You should be upset, but you stay in faith, and God opens up another door. A co-worker is playing politics, trying to make you look bad. You should try to get even. You should try to pay them back. But because of the anointing, your attitude isn't even affected. All that negativity just slides right off of you.

Many of you can look back and say with me, "I shouldn't be where I am today. How did I make it through the loss of my loved one? How did I make it through that slow season at work? How did I make it through that illness, that breakup, that accident, that addiction?" It was the anointing God put on your life. He gave you strength when you didn't think you could go on. He gave you joy when you should have been discouraged. He opened a door when it looked impossible.

You can say with David: If it had not been for the goodness of God, where would I be? (see Psalm 27:13). The bottom line is, God has infused His strength into you. He has equipped you and empowered you. You are ready for and equal to anything that comes your way. When you face tough times, remind yourself, "I'm not going to complain. I'm not going to get upset. I can handle it. I know God is still in control. He's fighting my battles. If God be for me, who dare be against me. I've been anointed for this."

You can say with David: If it had not been for the goodness of God, where would I be?

Say "no more" to fear:

Each of the four Gospels describes a scene in which Jesus is anointed. Matthew and Mark describe a woman pouring perfume on Jesus' head (see Matthew 26:6–13; Mark 14:1–9). Jesus says she did what she could, and people will be talking about it for the rest of time. Luke speaks of a sinful woman, anointing Jesus' feet out of an abundance of gratitude (see Luke 7:36–50). John relates a time when Mary, sister of Lazarus and Martha, anoints Jesus' feet with perfume, then wipes His feet with her hair (see John 12:1–8). In each case, there were people who didn't understand what was going on. It seemed like a waste to them. But each time, Jesus corrected them. There is a purpose in the anointing He said. He was being prepared for His death on the cross. He was anointed to do hard things.

Start living in faith:

▶ **APPLICATION**

Take a moment to look at nature. Find a spider's web, and admire its construction. Listen to the unique calls of different types of birds. Stop and watch ants carrying away a picnic. God cares for all of these creatures; how much more does He care for you?

▶ **DECLARATION**

I am anointed to do hard things. When life throws things at me, they won't stick because God's hand is upon me. I can handle anything that comes my way with strength and dignity because of the anointing.

▶ **PRAYER**

God, if it had not been for Your goodness, where would I be? You have anointed me to withstand the storms that come against me. I do not have to be afraid because I trust that if You bring me to it, You have anointed me for it. In Jesus' name, Amen.

CHAPTER 20

Faith Like A Bumblebee

When our children, Jonathan and Alexandra, were about three and six years old, we spent the day at the beach. We were having a good time making castles in the sand when a small bumblebee came and landed right beside us. Alexandra ran off afraid. I swatted him away. We went back to playing, but 30 seconds later, he was right back flying all around us.

The kids were screaming, "Daddy, get him!" I got a towel and I swatted him down to the ground. I thought I showed him who was boss. About a minute later, however, there he was again. This time I got my tennis shoe and squashed him into the sand as hard as I could. I was tired of dealing with him.

A couple of minutes later, I looked over to make sure he was still dead. I couldn't believe it. I saw one wing start to move. Soon he had the other wing out from under the sand. He walked around for a few seconds, dazed. I was amazed not only that he was alive, but that he could get back up again.

About that time, he took off into the air, flying away. Just when I thought I was finished with him, he turned back around and buzzed my head three or four times. I had to dodge him. This time when Alexandra said, "Daddy, get the towel; kill him!" I said, "No, Alexandra, this bumblebee deserves to live. I'm a thousand times bigger than him, and I still can't keep him down."

That's the way you need to see yourself. It doesn't matter how big the enemy looks. It doesn't matter how much stronger the adversary seems. There is a force in you that is more powerful than any opposition.

Greater is He who is in you than what comes against you. You need to act like that bumblebee and refuse to give up, refuse to get discouraged, refuse to give in to self-pity, and refuse to be overwhelmed. Instead, have the attitude, "With God on my side, nothing can keep me down." When you have this attitude, then all the forces of darkness cannot keep you from your destiny.

Some of you have already decided, "I can't handle this sickness. I can't deal with this problem at work. I can't take care of my elderly parents. I'll never get over this rejection." Quit telling yourself it's too much. Quit dwelling on those weak, defeated thoughts. Have faith like the bumblebee that no matter what comes against you, you will keep getting up. You will keep fighting back. You will keep on moving toward your destiny.

It doesn't matter how big the enemy looks. It doesn't matter how much stronger the adversary seems. There is a force in you that is more powerful than any opposition.

Say "no more" to fear:

▶ **REFLECTION**

It made no sense at all for David to take on Goliath (see 1 Samuel 17). David was not in the army — he was still a youth and watching his father's sheep. David was young, tiny compared to the giant Goliath, and had no experience with weapons. But David wasn't concerned with Goliath's size. He wasn't concerned with Goliath's sword. He knew that with God on his side, he couldn't lose. The same is true for you. What is in front you may be big — really big — but greater is He who is in you than any obstacle you will ever face.

Start living in faith:

▶ **APPLICATION**

When was the last time you faced an obstacle — or an opportunity — that seemed like it was too much for you? How did your faith react? Did you put your faith in your fears, or did your faith keep getting back up? The next chance you have to exercise your faith, remember that God will promote you, God will fight for you, and God will give you favor in the face of giants.

▶ **DECLARATION**

God is opening supernatural doors for me. I have favor in my home, in my relationships, in my career, and in my health. No giant is too big for me because God in me is greater than any obstacle I will face. Nothing can keep me down.

▶ **PRAYER**

God, thank You for giving me all the tools I need to fight my giants. Knowing that You are with me, I refuse to give up on these dreams; I refuse to get discouraged; I refuse to feel overwhelmed. You are mighty in me. In Jesus' name, Amen.

CHAPTER 21

The High Road

Often in life, fear shows up when we believe we have to protect or defend ourselves. But there is a key to operating free from fear, and it has to do with our own attitudes and actions. Paul said in Colossians 3:12 (NLT), *"Since God chose you to be the holy people he loves, you must clothe yourselves with tenderhearted mercy, kindness, humility, gentleness, and patience."* Clothing ourselves with these God-given virtues means that wherever we are, we have the power not to just be there, but to be there with the right attitude.

Are you being treated unfairly at work? It is one thing to go there sour, discouraged, complaining, and bad-mouthing the boss. That doesn't take much faith. But if you want to pass the test, you've got to be there with a good attitude. Put a smile on your face. Be kind to people. Do more than you have to.

Clothing ourselves with God-given virtues means that wherever we are, we have the power not to just be there, but to be there with the right attitude.

Has a friend suddenly turned on you? Are they making false accusations against you? It's natural to want to retaliate, to defend yourself, to point out their faults and mistakes. But God doesn't want us to respond in the natural; He wants us to respond in the supernatural. He wants us to turn the other cheek. He wants us to love our enemies and speak good about them. He wants us to leave our reputation up to Him.

In your home, if your spouse doesn't treat you right, it's easy to think, "I'm going to treat him the same way." Or if your kids are disrespectful, you might think, "I'm not going to give them more of my time." If you're going to pass the test, however, you've got to be good to people even when they're not being good to you. You've got to do the right thing, even and especially when the wrong thing is happening.

God wouldn't have allowed this difficulty if you couldn't handle it. See it as an opportunity to grow. When you do the right thing, there's a blessing that follows. When you take the high road, there will always be a reward.

The mistake we make too often is constantly telling ourselves, "This is not fair. This is not right. When they straighten up, then I'll have a better attitude. When this happens, then I'll be happy." No, you've got to make the first move. You do your part, and God will do His part. Quit worrying about God changing them, and let God change you. Take the high road.

Say "no more" to fear:

When Jacob met Rachel, it was love at first sight (see Genesis 29). He immediately asked her father, Laban, for her hand in marriage. They agreed that Jacob would work the farm for seven years, and then he could marry Rachel. After seven years, a wedding was planned. However, on the morning after the wedding, Jacob woke up next to Rachel's sister, Leah! Jacob could have stormed out. He could have bad-mouthed Laban all over town. He could have complained about how unfair the whole situation was. Instead, he worked another seven years with a good attitude, and the years went by as if they were only days. Because Jacob took the high road, he and his children were included in the lineage of Jesus. First Peter 5:6 (TLB) says, *"If you will humble yourselves under the mighty hand of God, in his good time he will lift you up."*

Start living in faith:

▶ **APPLICATION**

When you get dressed in the morning, imagine yourself putting on these virtues: compassion, kindness, humility, gentleness, and patience. Don't leave home until you are fully dressed and ready to take on the day with a good attitude!

▶ **DECLARATION**

I can handle anything that comes my way today. I can handle my plans not working out. I'll have a good attitude wherever I am.

▶ **PRAYER**

God, give me the strength to handle anything that comes my way today with a good attitude. I am dressed in patience and humility from head to toe. I am deciding ahead of time to take the high road. In Jesus' name, Amen.

CHAPTER 22

The Shaking Is For Shifting

In life, we all have times where things shake us to our core — an unexpected illness, a pandemic, economic uncertainty, losing a loved one, people who have been for us are suddenly against us. All the stability that we're used to — the finances we were counting on, the children doing great things — it's no longer there. It's easy to get discouraged and wonder why it happened. But here's the key: The shaking is not there to stop you; the shaking is there to shift you.

If you'll keep the right attitude, that shaking will shift you into promotion. It will shift you into greater influence. It will shift you into better relationships. You'll see divine connections, breakthroughs, and new opportunities. God uses these shakings to get us in position for new levels.

In Acts 16, Paul and Silas had been put in prison for sharing their faith. They were in the deepest dungeon, with chains around their feet. The authorities were so afraid of their influence, they went to great lengths to make sure Paul and Silas couldn't escape. You may be where Paul and Silas were. It may look like your situation doesn't have a solution, but God has ways of doing things that you've never thought of. At midnight, as Paul and Silas were singing praises to the Lord, *"suddenly there was a great earthquake; the prison was shaken to its foundations, all the doors flew open — and the chains of every prisoner fell off!"* (Acts 16:26, TLB). Notice what the shaking did. It opened prison doors. It loosed the chains that were restricting them. Paul and Silas walked out as free men.

The shaking on the surface may have seemed like a negative thing, but without the shaking, Paul wouldn't have fulfilled his purpose. The shaking was necessary for him to become who he was created to be. We may not like the shakings — the times when things are out of our control. In those times, remember: The shakings are not going to stop you; they're going to shift you.

Out of this shaking, new doors are going to open; new opportunities and new relationships will come your way. Chains that have held you back are about to be unfastened. Chains of depression, chains of lack and struggle, chains of addictions — you are being set free! Don't complain about the shaking; it's serving a purpose. God is using it to thrust you to where you couldn't go without it.

Without the door closing, we would never get out of our comfort zone. We may not like it, but the shaking is forcing us to change. It's forcing us to grow. If everything kept going along as is, we would never reach our potential. Stay open for something new. Don't go back to the same ways you used to do things. The reason God allowed the shaking is to shift you into something better.

In those times, remember: The shakings are not going to stop you; they're going to shift you.

Say "no more" to fear:

▶ **REFLECTION**

When Paul and Silas were put in prison, they had already been stripped and beaten. Then the jailer put them in "... *maximum security* ..." (Acts 16:24, MSG) and put their legs in stocks. How did they respond to the abuse, the injustice, and the extra security measures? By "... *praying and singing hymns to God* ..." (v. 25, NIV). Paul and Silas didn't wait until after the earthquake shook open the prison doors and set them free to praise God. They praised Him while they were still in chains. Don't wait until your miracle has come before you start praising God. Believe your day is coming and praise Him while you wait!

_____

_____

_____

_____

_____

_____

_____

_____

_____

_____

_____

_____

Start living in faith:

▶ **APPLICATION**

If you add your favorite candy to a bag of popcorn, what happens? Inevitably, the candy will fall to the bottom of the bag. What do you do? You shake it! What if God is shaking things up to get the good stuff to rise to the surface? The next time you feel shaken, thank God for shifting things in your life for His glory.

▶ **DECLARATION**

I know that even when things are shaking, it means it is because He is preparing for me something greater. No prison, no obstacle, and no barrier can hold me down. I will praise God in both the good times and the bad, just as I know He will be there for me in both, encouraging me to pursue the things He knows I am capable of.

▶ **PRAYER**

God, allow me the dedication to pursue my dreams even when things are shaking. Let Your strength push me forward even when obstacles threaten to stop me from doing so. Give me the patience to keep pursing the path You have set for me and the enduring strength to see it through.

CHAPTER 23

City Of Chaos; City Of Peace

In Acts 2, the disciples were in the upper room when the Holy Spirit came upon them like a mighty rushing wind. They were all filled with the Spirit. They knew God was with them, and they were going to do great things. But in chapter 8, a man named Saul came along. He hated these disciples. He had letters from the government to have them arrested and put in jail. The Scripture says in Acts 8:3 (NKJV), *"As for Saul, he made havoc of the church, entering every house, and dragging off men and women, committing them to prison."* He wreaked havoc on the church in Jerusalem.

Here the disciples were, preaching the Gospel, seeing God's favor, and out of nowhere Saul showed up and turned things upside down. Their whole world was shaken. It's interesting that Saul came to Jerusalem and

God is still on the throne. He's still ordering your steps. He has you in the palm of His hand.

caused so much turmoil. Jerusalem means "city of peace." This was home for many of the disciples. This is where they felt secure. They could relax and be comfortable. But Saul turned the city of peace into the city of chaos.

I'm sure the disciples thought, "God, where are You? Don't You see what Saul is doing?" Just a few chapters earlier, God had sent the mighty rushing wind. It's not like He couldn't have stopped Saul. He parted seas. He closed the mouths of lions. He could have kept Saul from ever entering Jerusalem. He could have sent angels to hold him back. But sometimes God will allow a Saul, a difficulty, an unfair situation, to get you to see things you've never seen before. Anyone can trust God when things are going their way. The real test is, will you trust Him when things are turned upside down? Will you stay in faith when there's uncertainty and things you don't understand?

Something or someone may have wreaked havoc in your life. Maybe things feel like they're out of control. Can I encourage you? God is still on the throne. He's still ordering your steps. He has you in the palm of His hand. Nothing can happen to you without His permission. He won't allow a difficulty to keep you from your destiny. God is working behind the scenes. Things are in motion that you can't see. One day you'll look back and say, "Wow, what I thought was a bad break was really setting me up for something new."

God promised that in this world we will have trouble. There will be times where things are unfair, turned upside, and we don't understand it. But that's not the time to fall apart. That's the time to kick your praise into a new gear. That's the time to speak victory over your life. That difficulty didn't come to stay — it came to pass. With God, you will get through this and come out better on the other side.

Say "no more" to fear:

On the surface, Saul probably thought that he had succeeded in breaking up the Church. But God wouldn't have allowed Saul to threaten His followers if He didn't have a larger purpose. When the believers scattered, they took with them the Good News about Jesus. They preached the Word and the Gospel spread to the ends of the earth like wildfire. When God allows something to come into your life, trust that He has a reason for it. You will come out better on the other side, and His name will be glorified.

Start living in faith:

▶ **APPLICATION**

Do you trust God in times of chaos, or only in times of peace? If life feels chaotic right now, take a praise break. Thank God that He is positioning you for something new, something bigger and better than where you currently are. If you are in a season of peace, consider how you got there. Did you have to come through the chaos to get to where you are?

▶ **DECLARATION**

Nothing I face will be too much for me. I will overcome every obstacle, outlast every challenge, and come through the chaos into a season of peace. God is working behind the scenes to propel me into my destiny.

▶ **PRAYER**

God, Your Word is full of the promise of peace. You say I can come to You and enter Your rest. You say that Your peace passes understanding. Lord, give me Your peace. Bring me through this season of chaos, stronger, better, and closer to my destiny. In Jesus' name, Amen.

CHAPTER 24

Great Difficulty Precedes Great Favor

I n Acts 8, Saul created so much havoc in Jerusalem that the disciples scattered. Verse 5 says that Philip went to Samaria. It wasn't by choice. It wasn't because he prayed for God to expand his territory. He was forced out of Jerusalem through the persecution of Saul.

Philip could have been discouraged. He could have been homesick. He could have whined and complained, but he understood that God was still in control. What's interesting is, Samaria is where Philip's ministry took off. Samaria is where he flourished and stepped into a new level. The Scripture says that Philip saw all kinds of miracles in Samaria. Blind eyes were opened, the crippled could walk, and great favor was on his life. Philip never saw that in Jerusalem. If he would have stayed there, he would have missed the fullness of his destiny. Many times great difficulty precedes great favor; great opposition precedes great influence.

I've learned when one door closes, if you'll stay in faith, God will open a bigger and better door. You may get pushed out of your Jerusalem, but Samaria is waiting for you. There's a place of victory, a place of abundance that God has already prepared for you. There are divine connections — people who God has already ordained to come into your life, people who will love you, people who can't wait to be with you. The enemy may have meant it to harm you, but he doesn't have the final say. God wouldn't have allowed that door to close if it was going to stop your purpose. Have a new perspective. God has more in store for you.

Acts 8:8 (NIV) says there was "... *great joy* ..." in Samaria. Philip left Jerusalem in great distress, but great joy was waiting for him. He went from great trouble to great victory; from great rejection to people who loved him deeply. You may have gone through things that have caused you great pain, great disappointment, and great loss. You could be bitter and live discouraged, but that is not how your story ends. Like with Philip, great joy is coming. Great favor, great relationships, and great health are in your future. You may not be there yet, but stay encouraged. You are headed toward great joy.

Quit being discouraged over what happened to you. If you could see what God is up to, you wouldn't be stressed, complaining, or upset. When you realize it's taking you to Samaria — a place where you're going to flourish, where you will do things you never dreamed, see favor, abundance, and breakthroughs you never imagined — then you will want to thank God even in the disruptions. Keep the right perspective. God is up to something good!

You may not be
there yet, but
stay encouraged.
You are headed
toward great joy.

Say "no more" to fear:

▶ **REFLECTION**

In Acts 8, we read about Philip's success in Samaria. After being pushed out of Jerusalem by Saul's antics, it is in Samaria that Philip discovers his gift as an evangelist. Then along comes an angel who tells Philip to "... *Go south* ..." (v. 26, NIV). Philip immediately obeys, heading down the desert road toward Gaza. Along the way, he meets an Ethiopian eunuch who was just traveling home in his chariot reading Scripture. Philip opens the Scripture to him, and the man is baptized into the faith. This scene epitomizes that the Gospel is for everyone — no matter where you are from or where you are now, no matter the color of your skin or your physical condition — all you have to do is believe. Because Philip didn't give up after being persecuted by Saul, he was able to be part of the Ethiopian's conversion story.

Start living in faith:

▶ **APPLICATION**

Have you ever been pushed out of your Jerusalem? Have you been over-looked for a promotion? Have you done all the right things, said all the right things and gone to church every week, but your plans for adoption still fell through? Were you rejected when you got down on one knee? Shift your focus from your Jerusalem — from the plans that you had for your life — and turn them towards your Samaria. Believe that God is doing something behind the scenes, opening doors, and bringing you favor so that you can flourish.

▶ **DECLARATION**

This is not the end; it's only the beginning. God is opening doors that no man can shut. I am entering a new season where I will flourish. God's favor is upon me. What He has for me is filled with great joy.

▶ **PRAYER**

Father, I don't understand what You are doing behind the scenes, but I trust You when You say that great joy is coming. I believe that You closed that door to protect me from a mediocre life. There is more in store. Use me for Your glory. In Jesus' name, Amen.

CHAPTER 25

More Than Enough

God is looking for people whose hearts are turned toward Him — people like you; people who honor Him; people who keep Him first place. Psalm 37:19 (NLT) says, *". . . even in famine they will have more than enough."* Not just enough, but more than enough — abundance, overflow, plenty. There are blessings that are going to come looking for you.

If we put our trust in our finances, they can go down like that. If we put our trust in our job, our career, it can suddenly change. That's why it's so important to put your trust in God. He's the One who doesn't change. He's our Source. That's where we get strength, ideas, creativity, resources, and wisdom. God is the giver of all good things.

I talked to a lady who watches us on television. She owns her own business and has stores all over the country. A few years ago, her business was struggling. It was barely surviving. One day, she received word that 36 of her stores were closing. That was almost half of her business. She couldn't make it without that income. She could have accepted it and given up on her dream. But in the middle of all the uncertainty, she said, "God, I trust You. I know You're still in control. You can make a way where I don't see a way." A few weeks later, a large company called and said they wanted to put her product in 360 of their stores. Almost overnight she went from 36 stores to 360.

I've learned that God is not so much into addition; He's more into multiplication. One touch of His favor will catapult you ahead. We look at our circumstances in the natural and think this could never work out, but we serve a supernatural God. He's not limited by what limits us. One good break, one contract, one phone call, one divine favor, and God will multiply what you have. He'll thrust you to a new level.

If everything is against you right now, it's a sign that God is about to shift things. There's going to be shift in your finances, a shift in your career, a shift in your health, a shift in your marriage. It's shaky right now, things seem uncertain, you're tempted to worry and live stressed; but a shift is coming. God is going to make things happen that you couldn't make happen. Instead of being stressed over your problems, start thanking Him that He has already provided the solution.

Instead of being stressed
over your problems, start
thanking Him that He has
already provided the solution.

Say "no more" to fear:

▶ **REFLECTION**

Matthew 14 says that Jesus had been preaching and healing all day. His disciples were getting tired as dinnertime was approaching. They suggested that Jesus "...*send the crowds away*..." (v. 15, NIV) so that they could get something to eat. But Jesus said, "...*That isn't necessary — you feed them*" (v. 16, NLT). The disciples looked at what they had in the natural — five loaves of bread and two fish — as if to say, "No way; it's not enough!" But we don't serve a God of not-enough. We serve a God of plenty, of abundance, of more than enough. Jesus blessed the food and gave it back to the disciples to pass out to the crowds. And you know what? They ended up with more food than what they started with.

Start living in faith:

▶ **APPLICATION**

God gives generously to us so that we can give generously to others — we are blessed to be a blessing! Where has God blessed you with more than enough? What do you have an abundance of that you can give to others? Maybe it is time or money; maybe it is forgiveness or grace; maybe it is wisdom or encouragement. God lavishes these gifts on us so that we can pour out His love on others. Be intentional this week as you look for opportunities to give cheerfully and abundantly to those in need.

▶ **DECLARATION**

I live in the land of plenty. I do not live in lack. I have more than enough. My God goes exceedingly, abundantly, and above and beyond every single time for me. He is multiplying favor in my life.

▶ **PRAYER**

Father, thank You that a shift is coming. Breakthroughs, healing, favor, and opportunities are on their way. Thank You that what You started in my life, You will finish in victory. In Jesus' name, Amen.

CHAPTER 26

Created To Shine

God has put gifts and talents in you. He's given you dreams and goals that are unique to your life. You have something to offer that nobody else has. But it's easy to let fear hold us back — fear of failure, fear of what people are going to think, fear of the unknown. "What if I try it and it doesn't work? What if people don't accept me? What if I don't have the talent?" Too often we let the "what ifs" talk us out of our destiny.

Many people are living with hidden dreams, hidden talent, and hidden potential. They have book ideas, songs, businesses, leadership skills, and ministries in them that they haven't developed. They've discounted themselves, thinking they're not as talented as their friends; they've had too many setbacks; they tried in the past, and it didn't work out.

"No one lights a lamp and then covers it with a bowl or hides it under a bed. A lamp is placed on a stand, where its light can be seen by all who enter the house."

LUKE 8:16 (NLT)

The Scripture says, *"No one lights a lamp and then covers it with a bowl or hides it under a bed. A lamp is placed on a stand, where its light can be seen by all who enter the house"* (Luke 8:16, NLT). When God breathed His life into you, He lit your candle. He created you to shine, to make a difference, to leave your mark. Your gift isn't just for you; it's to share with the world. We need your talent; we need your creativity; we need your smile. Stop telling yourself you can't do it. God wouldn't have given you that dream if He had not equipped you to achieve it.

You can't play it safe your whole life and become who you were created to be. God will put you in situations on purpose that look overwhelming. It's because He knows what's in you. He knows what you're capable of. He created you. Deep down you know you're supposed to step out; you know that gift is in you, but you're afraid.

When you take a step of faith, that gift will come to life, and you'll discover ability that you didn't know you had. But here's the key: You can't wait till the fear goes away and then do it. The fear may never go away. You're going to have to do it in spite of the fear. That's what faith is all about.

You have gifts in you right now that you don't know you have. God has hidden them until the right time. We go through seasons of preparation, when our gifts are developed behind the scenes. But in due season, you'll know in your spirit, it's your time to shine.

Say "no more" to fear:

In Isaiah 49, the prophet Isaiah lamented that he felt like he'd "... *labored in vain* ..." (v. 4, NIV). He'd been working so hard, using his gifts, following God's lead, but for what? God reassures him, "... *I will make you a Light to the nations* ..." (Isaiah 49:6, TLB). We don't always see the results of our efforts. We don't always see the impact we are making. But that's not really the point. The point is to be faithful to the call God has placed on your life. The point is to use all of the gifts and talents that God has given you, walk through all the doors that God has opened for you, and let your light shine bright. Then, like Isaiah, you can say, "... *Yet I leave it all in the* Lord's *hand; I will trust God for my reward*" (v. 4, NLT).

_____

_____

_____

_____

_____

_____

_____

_____

_____

_____

_____

_____

_____

_____

Start living in faith:

▶ **APPLICATION**

If God has given you the gift to sing, start singing. If you can write, start writing. If you can lead, start leading. If you can build, start building. If you can teach, start teaching. That gift wasn't meant to stay hidden. If you do so, it doesn't do you any good, and it's certainly not doing the world any good if you keep it to yourself. It has to be released.

▶ **DECLARATION**

I was created to shine. I was created to leave my mark. God has a unique plan for my life — something only I can do. I will not live in fear. I will not hide my light. I'm going to let it shine!

▶ **PRAYER**

God, thank You for the gifts and talents You have put in me. Give me the faith to step out and use my gifts to make the world a better, brighter place. It's my time to shine! In Jesus' name, Amen.

CHAPTER 27

Enemy Tactics

When you get close to releasing your gift, you'll feel more fear than ever. That's the enemy trying to deceive you into keeping your gift hidden. He doesn't want you to step into a new level. He doesn't want you to shine and go where no one in your family has gone. He doesn't want you to take new ground for the Kingdom. He'll work overtime to try to convince you to shrink back and play it safe. You're going to have to have boldness and courage that you've never had before.

"What if I fail?" You get up and try again. Every failure is preparing you. You can't be so afraid of failure that you don't get out of your comfort zone. You will learn more through failure than through success, more in the difficult times than in the good times.

Thomas Edison made 10,000 attempts before he finally invented the light bulb. A reporter asked him about all of his failures. He said, "I never failed; I just learned 10,000 ways a light bulb wouldn't work." Even when it doesn't work out, you're learning, you're growing, and you're one step closer to seeing it happen.

When we come to the end of life, nothing will be more disappointing than to think, "What would have happened if I would have taken that step of faith? What could I have become if I hadn't let fear hold me back? Where would I be if I wouldn't have hidden my talent, hidden my dreams, hidden my gifts?" Friends, life is short. Stir up what God put in you. Make the most of this day. Don't let fear of failure, fear of what people are going to think, or fear of being criticized hold you back.

"Well, Joel, I don't want anyone to judge me. I don't want people to talk bad about me." Can I tell you, people are going to talk about you whether you settle or whether you stretch. You might as well stretch and pursue what God put in your heart.

Quit worrying about who's not for you. Some enemies are designed as a part of your destiny. You'll never please everyone. You can't keep all your friends, relatives, and co-workers happy. If you try, the one person who won't be happy is you. Other people may not see your gift. They don't know what God's put in you. They can't feel what you feel. Don't let their discouragement talk you out of it. Don't let the fear of what they think hold you back. You're not going to give an account to people of what you did with your life; you're going to give an account to God (see Romans 14:12).

Friends, life is short. Stir up what God put in you. Make the most of this day.

Say "no more" to fear:

One of the best things I've learned is that everybody is not supposed to be for you. Not everybody is supposed to like you. You can't reach your destiny without opposition, without critics, and without negative chatter. Joseph wouldn't have made it to the throne without his brothers betraying him. David would have never become king without Goliath. Jesus would have never risen from the dead and brought us salvation without Judas betraying him. God can use the enemy's tactics to propel you into your destiny.

Start living in faith:

▶ APPLICATION

Is the enemy attacking you right now? Does it feel like the entire world is against you? Congratulations! You are on the verge of doing great things. Don't give up right on the brink of your breakthrough. Dig deep. Pray and praise God. Keep in faith, trusting that this setback is a setup for your destiny.

▶ DECLARATION

The enemy is attacking me because he knows what is in me. I will not bow down to fear. God is using this trial to strengthen me. I am taking ground for the Kingdom. I am bold and courageous. I am learning. I am growing. I am one step closer to success.

▶ PRAYER

God, You are greater than the enemy that is attacking me. Fear has no part in my life. Thank You for strengthening me in this season against the enemy's attacks. I trust that You are bringing me into victory. In Jesus' name, Amen.

CHAPTER 28

Buried Dreams

In Matthew 25, Jesus told a parable about a businessman who was going on a trip. He called three employees over. He gave one five talents, another two talents, and the third, one talent. A talent represented 20 years' worth of wages. It was a significant amount of money.

The man with five talents went out, invested it, and made five more. The one with two invested his and made two more. But the one with one talent was afraid. He thought, "What if I lose it? What if the economy goes down? What if somebody steals it from me?" He came up with all these excuses of what could happen, so he went and buried his talent in the ground.

You and I have been given gifts. God has entrusted us with them. . . . What are you doing with what you have?

The man with five talents and the man with two talents based their investments on faith. But the man with one talent based his response on fear. You'll never increase as long as you're living a fear-based life.

All three men had the same opportunity. Two did something with their gifts, while the other played it safe. When the owner returned, the first man said, "Here are the five talents you gave me, plus five more." The owner said, "Well done." The second man said, "Here are the two original talents, plus two more." Again, the owner said, "Well done."

Finally, the owner came to the third man who said, "*. . . I knew that you are a hard man, harvesting where you have not sown and gathering where you have not scattered seed. So I was afraid and went out and hid your gold in the ground. See, here is what belongs to you*" (Matthew 25:24–25, NIV). You might think the owner would be happy to get back what he gave, but it was just the opposite. This owner was expecting a profit. He expected increase. He called the man wicked and lazy, took his one talent away, and gave it to the man who had five.

The owner in this parable represents God. This is some of the strongest language used in the Scripture. It's interesting that the man didn't lie, he didn't cheat, he didn't take somebody's life, and he didn't have an affair. What did he do? He buried his talent. He hid what God gave him. You and I have been given gifts. God has entrusted us with them. One day He's going to come back and ask, "What did you do with the talents I gave you?" Whether you have one, two, or five, that doesn't matter. What matters is what are you doing with what you have?

Say "no more" to fear:

▶ **REFLECTION**

A group of businesspeople were discussing where the wealthiest place in the world is. One of them said, "It has to be South Africa in the diamond mines, where there are billions of dollars of diamonds and jewels." Another said, "No, it must be in the oil fields of the Middle East, where they have an abundance of oil." But the truth is that the wealthiest place on the earth is not South Africa. Nor is it the Middle East. Sadly, it's in the graveyards. In those graves are buried dreams — books that were never written, songs that were never sung, businesses that were never started, inventions that were never invented, and relationships that were never formed. Instead of burying your dreams, it's time to start burying your fears. Bury the insecurity, bury the doubt, bury the negative thoughts, bury what the critics have said, and start showing your talent, your skill, and your smile.

Start living in faith:

▶ **APPLICATION**

What are you doing with your talents? Are you living fear-based, afraid to take a risk, not willing to get out of your comfort zone, not putting in the effort to develop your gift? Or are you living faith-based, growing, stretching, looking for opportunities, developing what you have, and believing you have seeds of greatness?

▶ **DECLARATION**

I am developing my talents. I am pursuing my dreams. I am cultivating my gifts. God has gifted me, and I will not take that lightly. I will not bury my dreams. I will bury my fears and use every gift God has given me.

▶ **PRAYER**

God, You did not put these dreams in my heart for me to bury them. You have gifted me with all things I need to succeed in life. Help me to live a faith-based life. In Jesus' name, Amen.

CHAPTER 29

Small Gifts, Great Potential

Too often we discount ourselves, thinking we don't have much to offer. We look at what we don't have and what we can't do. Your gift may seem small, but if you'll start using it, it will grow. It's like an acorn. You could look at it and think, "Big deal. All I have is this little gift. God, You created the universe, and this is all You've given me?" What you can't see is, there is incredible potential in that small gift. In that little acorn is a huge oak tree.

Proverbs 18:16 (NKJV) says, *"A man's gift makes room for him. . . ."* It doesn't say a big gift, an important gift, or an impressive gift. Whatever you have, if you'll develop it and keep getting better, it will open doors of opportunity, doors of promotion, and doors of influence.

In the Scripture, Gideon was hiding in the winepress, afraid of his enemies, when God told him to go tear down an idol (see Judges 6). Gideon refused to go in the daytime. He was too fearful, so he went at night. Later, God said Gideon was to deliver the people of Israel from the Midianites — the same people who Gideon had been hiding from in the winepress.

Gideon responded, ". . . *How can I rescue Israel? My clan is the weakest in the whole tribe of Manasseh, and I am the least in my entire family!*" (Judges 6:15, NLT). He was saying, "My gift is too small."

An angel had said to him, ". . . *Mighty hero, the* LORD *is with you!*" (Judges 6:12, NLT). Here Gideon was, hiding, afraid and feeling inadequate, yet God called him a mighty hero. Your gift may seem small. You may feel unqualified. The obstacles look too big. But God is saying to you what He said to Gideon, "Hello, you mighty hero. I have big plans for you." God sees what you can become.

God gave Gideon favor. Gideon and his 300 men went out and defeated the Midianites, an army of over 130,000 people. Gideon went on to become a great leader. Today he's listed as one of the heroes of faith (see Hebrews 11:32). If Gideon would have stayed in hiding, if he would have stayed convinced that his gifts were too small, he would have missed his destiny.

I'm asking you to come out of hiding. Like Gideon, you're going to accomplish dreams that look impossible. Talent is going to come out that you didn't know you had. Doors are going to open that you couldn't open. You're going to rise higher, overcome obstacles, and reach the fullness of your destiny. Your gift may seem small, but when you develop it, big doors will open.

Your gift may seem small, but when you develop it, big doors will open.

Say "no more" to fear:

Out in the shepherds' fields, David could have thought, "God, all I'm good at is slinging rocks with this slingshot. Why didn't You give me more talent?" Instead, David kept developing that small gift. He kept practicing and getting better until he could hit a bull's eye 100 feet away. One day, he faced Goliath — a giant twice his size. Goliath was wearing armor that covered his whole body — every part except around his eyes and forehead. David picked up a stone and put it in his slingshot. When he slung it, it hit Goliath right in the forehead. Goliath fell dead to the ground, and David became a national hero, all because he was willing to work with that small gift.

Start living in faith:

▶ **APPLICATION**

Like David, Gideon was the smallest one in his family. Unlike David, Gideon let it bother him. Gideon didn't immediately respond to God's call with bravery, but God didn't give up on him. If you've been hiding in fear, you haven't missed your opportunity. God still has a plan for your life. God still calls you a "mighty hero." Start with baby steps, if you have to, as you begin to step out in faith into all that God has for you.

▶ **DECLARATION**

The Lord is with me. He has big plans for my life. The potential is already in me. I will not discount my gifts because they seem small. I am a mighty hero, prepared to do good works.

▶ **PRAYER**

God, thank You for seeing me not as I am today but as who I can become and who You created me to be. Help me to not look down on the "small" gifts in my life but to see their potential for growth. I want to be faithful with all of the gifts that You have given me. In Jesus' name, Amen.

CHAPTER 30

That One Thing

Paul said in Philippians 3:13 (TLB), *"No, dear brothers, I am still not all I should be, but I am bringing all my energies to bear on this one thing: Forgetting the past and looking forward to what lies ahead."* All of his energy, all of his focus was on one thing — and one thing only.

What could you accomplish if you weeded out everything that wasn't moving you toward your destiny? Where could you be at this time next year if you got rid of the distractions and all that isn't producing good fruit? What would happen if you put all your efforts into the main thing that you know God has put in your heart?

Studies show that when a person spends 10,000 hours doing the same thing, they become an expert. Find that one thing and do it to the best of

God is creative, so you are creative.
God is wise, so you are wise. God is
powerful, so you are powerful.

your ability. It may mean taking a class online, getting your finances in order so you can start that business, or finding a mentor who you can learn from to develop your skills. It may mean cutting down on your screen time, quitting a job, or letting go of a hobby in this season. You may be able to do many things good, but you can't do many things great. We can spread ourselves too thin. That's why Paul said, this "*. . . one thing I do. . . .*" Find that one thing for you, and excel at it.

When God created you, He put a part of Himself in you. God is creative, so you are creative. God is wise, so you are wise. God is powerful, so you are powerful. God is good-looking, so you are good-looking. (I've never seen Him, but I thought I might as well throw that one in!) I've learned that you can talk yourself out of your dreams, or you can talk yourself into your dreams.

Quit telling yourself you can't do it, you don't have the right personality, you don't have the training, you don't have the time, or you'll do it later. Get rid of those excuses, and start telling yourself what God says about you: You are strong, you are talented, you are favored, and you are blessed. You have been fearfully and wonderfully made.

God doesn't choose the way we choose. He doesn't always go find the smartest, most gifted, or most experienced person to carry out His will. He's looking for willing hearts — people whose energy is focused on that one thing He has uniquely created for them to do in this world. It's not how much you have; it's what you are doing with what you have that matters to Him. Find your one thing, and throw all of your energy into it!

Say "no more" to fear:

▶ **REFLECTION**

Two of the most famous sisters in Scripture are Mary and Martha. Jesus loved to dine with them and their brother Lazarus. One day, while Jesus was there for supper, Mary sat at His feet and listened to His stories, while Martha fretted in the kitchen. When she'd finally had enough, Martha came to Jesus to complain about her lazy sister. Instead of taking her side, Jesus said, ". . . *Martha, Martha, you are worried and troubled about many things*" (Luke 10:41, NKJV). He continued, "*There is really only one thing worth being concerned about. Mary has discovered it — and I won't take it away from her!*" (v. 42, TLB). Martha had allowed the "many things" to distract her from the "one thing" that was worth worrying about — spending time with Jesus.

Start living in faith:

▶ **APPLICATION**

What is distracting you from that one thing that God wants you to pursue in life? What is one thing you can do today to start eliminating those distractions? Write down that one thing that God wants you to focus on. Put it somewhere that you can see it every day. Remind yourself to put all your energy and all your focus into that one thing.

▶ **DECLARATION**

I am putting all of my energy into that one thing that God has for me. I will focus on this one thing. I would rather do this one thing great than a lot of things well. I will not settle for a mediocre life. That one thing is my destiny.

▶ **PRAYER**

God, I am grateful for who You are in my life and all that You have done for me. I want to do great things for You, but I can't do that if I'm too spread out. Help me to set aside distractions and focus on that one thing You have especially for me. In Jesus' name, Amen.

ABOUT JOEL OSTEEN MINISTRIES

Joel Osteen Ministries, rooted in Houston, Texas, is an extension of the legacy built by John and Dodie Osteen, who founded Lakewood Church in 1959. Originally meeting in a modest feed store, Lakewood has grown into one of the largest congregations in the U.S., attracting people from all walks of life. John Osteen's leadership touched millions through his television ministry, which reached over 100 countries, and his influence as a pastor's pastor. His wife, Dodie, also played a key role, especially with her testimony of miraculous healing from cancer, which has inspired countless people.

When John passed away in 1999, his son Joel stepped into leadership, despite his background in television production. Joel's transition into senior pastor marked a new era for Lakewood, with the church's global influence expanding significantly. Under Joel's leadership, Lakewood's outreach grew, broadcasting to over 200 million households, and the church became a beacon of hope for millions seeking encouragement and inspiration.

Joel's wife, Victoria, serves alongside him, contributing to the church's leadership and vision. Their daughter, Alexandra, continues the family tradition, leading worship and contributing to Lakewood Music. With a focus on uplifting messages and practical teachings, Joel Osteen Ministries aims to reach new generations, inspiring people worldwide to rise above their challenges and live their best life through faith, hope, and love.

Stay encouraged *and* inspired all through the week.

Download the Joel Osteen Daily Podcast *and* **subscribe now** *on* **YouTube to get the latest videos.**

For a full listing, visit **JoelOsteen.com/How-To-Watch**.

Stay connected, *be* blessed.

Get more from Joel & Victoria Osteen

It's time to step into the life of victory and favor that God has planned for you! Featuring new messages from Joel & Victoria Osteen, their free daily devotional, and inspiring articles, hope is always at your fingertips with the free Joel Osteen app and online at JoelOsteen.com.

Get the app and visit us today at JoelOsteen.com.

 JOEL OSTEEN MINISTRIES

CONNECT WITH US